# The Project Management Communications Toolkit

DISCLAIMER OF WARRANTY

The technical descriptions, procedures, and computer programs in this book have been developed with the greatest of care and they have been useful to the author in a broad range of applications; however, they are provided as is, without warranty of any kind. Artech House, Inc. and the author and editors of the book titled *The Project Management Communications Toolkit* make no warranties, expressed or implied, that the equations, programs, and procedures in this book or its associated software are free of error, or are consistent with any particular standard of merchantability, or will meet your requirements for any particular application. They should not be relied upon for solving a problem whose incorrect solution could result in injury to a person or loss of property. Any use of the programs or procedures in such a manner is at the user's own risk. The editors, author, and publisher disclaim all liability for direct, incidental, or consequent damages resulting from use of the programs or procedures in this book or the associated software.

For a listing of recent titles in the *Artech House Effective Project Management Library,* turn to the back of this book.

# The Project Management Communications Toolkit

Carl Pritchard

Artech House, Inc.
Boston • London
www.artechhouse.com

Library of Congress Cataloging-in-Publication Data
Pritchard, Carl L.
    The project management communications toolkit / Carl Pritchard.
      p. cm. – (Artech House project management library)
    ISBN 1-58053-747-2 (alk. paper)
    1. Management information systems. 2. Project management. I. Title II. Series.

    T58.6.P736 2004
    658.4'038–dc22                      2004041033


British Library Cataloguing in Publication Data
Pritchard, Carl
The project management communications toolkit
    1. Communication in management    2. Project management
    I. Title
    658.4'5

    ISBN 1-58053-747-2

Cover design by Igor Valdman

International Standard Book Number: 1-58053-747-2

10 9 8 7 6 5 4 3 2 1

# Contents

## CHAPTER 4

Communications Tools in the Planning Processes                     67

# Preface

"What's a risk plan look like?"

"Have you ever hosted a closeout meeting before?"

Those are the questions that students have put to me time and again, and the impetus behind this book. All too often, managers in general and project managers specifically are called on to generate forms, formats, and approaches that are alien to them. They surf, borrow, and steal what they can, but they are not necessarily getting the full understanding of how, why, and when the approaches are to be used. This book serves as a compendium of classic approaches organized accordingly to the Project Management Institute's *Guide to the Project Management Body of Knowledge* processes.

Also, as technology evolves, new approaches that may have been avant-garde just a few years ago are rapidly becoming more commonplace. Those have been addressed here as well. Each approach is coupled with a tool, template, or process, and a description of what it is, how it is used, when it is best applied, and the considerations that may be taken into account in using it.

The real driving force behind this text was Bob Wysocki, a respected colleague working to advance the literature base in project management. He provided extensive up-front insight on what the book should and should not include and how to structure it for ease of use. My thanks also to Delaine Campbell for her gifted insight on content, arrangement, and project management practice.

I also wish to thank Artech House and their team of professionals for their direct contributions to making this a better book. Christine Daniele, Mark Walsh, and Judi Stone were invaluable in initiating the project and ensuring that it got off the ground successfully. Editors Barbara Lovenvirth and Rebecca Allendorf, very patient souls, challenged the work as appropriate and provided fresh sets of eyes to scour the content. They contributed significantly in rendering effective professional guidance.

My thanks to you, the reader, as well, for your investment of time, effort, and money in purchasing this text. If you have suggestions, contributions, or insights on how to improve this or similar works in the future, I welcome them. My office e-mail is carl@carlpritchard.com.

## CHAPTER 1

# The Nature of Project Communications

Communication is the cornerstone of effective project management, and yet most of it is done ad hoc, driven by individuals, personalities, and preferences, rather than by needs, protocols, processes, and procedures. Communication breakdowns are continuously cited as one of the key reasons that projects fail, which is why communication needs to be addressed as a critical activity and skill for project managers.

The rationale for this book is that it will help managers improve or enhance their communications. But "improving communications" is an amorphous concept. No two people are going to have the same notion as to what that means, unless communications goals are identified on the project. Communication is, as David Acker [1] put it, an effort to make the world "smaller." It is an attempt to create a common understanding and a common informational basis among various parties. It is the pursuit of commonality. In Latin, the prefix *com-* means "together." It is an effort to bring individuals closer together.

How close is appropriate in the project environment? How deep must the common understanding be? The goal of communication in the project environment needs to be to establish a common understanding *to the requisite level of depth*. That level of depth will vary from project stakeholder to stakeholder. A security guard who affords access into the building may need only a single memo or e-mail from time to time, and needs virtually no understanding of the project plan or its intricacies. The customer needs to know what is being delivered and when, but may have no need to know *how* the work is being performed. Internal managers may need information on resource usage and performance, but may not concern themselves with project performance from day to day.

As a general practice, the goal of communication should be to clarify information to the level of depth required by the receiver by minimizing barriers that might inhibit understanding. In implementation, that implies a broad understanding of audience, interest, and environment.

Done properly, good communications change the entire project experience for the better. Effective communications can and will build more lasting customer relationships, expedite activities, and keep projects in control by ensuring that responsible parties are aware of what they need to be aware of when they need to be aware of it. Good communications are consistent. That is not to say that communications modes and styles won't be different from communicator to communicator, but for each communicator, there will be certain expectations of consistency.

To see the downside of poor communication, one need look no further than the space shuttle *Challenger* disaster in 1986. One of the primary reasons cited for the disaster was the failure of the O-rings to protect the seals on the solid rocket booster. The O-rings failed despite repeated communication between NASA and Morton Thiokol regarding concerns about the potential for O-ring failure. Meetings, teleconferences, and memoranda all failed to generate sufficient concern that the launch was in jeopardy [2].

When communications are effective, the results can be equally powerful. The September 11, 2001, tragedy could have been far worse for Morgan Stanley in their World Trade Center facility had their vice president of security not been a powerful and effective communicator. Rick Rescorla's communications skills were made evident by the fact that after the garage of the World Trade Center was bombed in 1993, Rescorla was able to drag investment bankers and brokers through regular evacuation drills. These are not individuals easily torn away from their work. When the World Trade Center was hit by the first jet on September 11, 2001, Morgan Stanley personnel in three of the WTC's seven buildings evacuated, while those in other organizations stayed behind. Clear communications made their evacuation activities rote. The Morgan Stanley personnel knew what to do because it had been communicated to them consistently by someone with conviction about the message. As a result, thousands of additional lives were saved [3].

Granted, most project managers don't get the opportunity to launch shuttles or rescue personnel trapped in burning buildings, but communications are part and parcel of the day-to-day activities of a project manager. The Project Management Institute recognizes that on their certification exam for project professionals. The exam cites that 90% of the project manager's time is invested in communication [4]. Most of that time is not invested in dramatic presentations or meetings with powerful executives. It is invested instead in the simple direction of the project, guiding team members as they go about their responsibilities, or responding to customer requests.

That simple direction is not only one-on-one communications. The Project Management Institute's 2003 "Project of the Year" award went to the organizers of the 2002 Winter Olympic Games in Salt Lake City, Utah. Eighteen project managers had to coordinate their efforts to lead a staff of almost 48,000 workers [5]. Such efforts require expansive coordination and consistency in communication. Similar forms and formats must be used. Clear, guiding messages must be sent.

Even on smaller projects, clear communications become essential. Anyone who has arranged a retirement party or wedding knows the negative consequences that can ensue if the caterer and the owner of the facility hosting the event are not given consistent data. Egos may be bruised and critical steps and responsibilities may be overlooked.

One-on-one communication is relatively simple and clear. That's because there is only one recipient to the message—there is only one other person on the other side of the equation. But as more and more participants are engaged, the challenges in communications and communications planning increase geometrically. The mathematical models for calculating the number of communications channels can be presented in two ways. Consider the following equation, where $n$ represents the number of participants in the communications process:

$$\frac{n*(n-1)}{2} \quad \text{or} \quad \frac{n^2 - n}{2}$$

Both formulas yield the same result. If there are three team members, there are three lines of communication that must be maintained if everyone is to have the same level of information. If there are 30 team members, 435 channels must be maintained. The shifts in the number of channels to be maintained increase dramatically with team size.

This becomes a consideration in the types of tools to be applied in the communication. Interviews are fine and appropriate with a smaller team. With a team of 15 or more, such interviews may become unwieldy, because sharing the information consistently across the body of stakeholders is a challenge. Forms and formats that encourage consistency become progressively more desirable the larger a team becomes.

## The Role of the Project Manager in Communications

The role of the project manager is one of communications facilitator. That does not mean he or she sends all of the communications. It means that the project manager is responsible for ensuring that communications are sent, received, and (to the degree possible) understood. To accomplish that, the project manager can identify preferred communications modes for the critical stakeholders, assess the best means to enable those modes, and ensure the integrity of the process as the project continues.

To identify preferred communications modes, the project manager should assess a representative sample of the project's stakeholders. In a small project, this may be done by interviews. In larger projects, this may be accomplished by surveys. The process and questions are discussed further in the section on the communications plan tool (Chapter 4).

Once the communications modes have been identified, the next task in the communications plan—enabling those communications modes is critical. The project manager may need to establish e-mail protocols or telephone voice-mail etiquette. He or she may need to invest time and energy in constructing a project Web site or "virtual community" on the *local-area network* (LAN). He or she may need to identify the specific tools to be used (and tools to be avoided) based on customer and team needs. Regardless of the choice of technology or approach, guidance needs to be established to ensure consistent application. Without consistency, communications will eventually break down.

To ensure the integrity of the process, the project manager must test the system occasionally to ensure that messages are being received and understood. In one training organization, the president would occasionally plant brief, bizarre messages deep in his memoranda to test whether or not the entire message was being received. He learned that only a handful of his staff were really reading the entire document, and he changed his protocols as a result. The project manager who communicates well will find ways to test the integrity of the system, both in terms of message receipt and understanding. Just because an e-mail is marked as "received" doesn't ensure that it was actually read *or* understood. Validation through spot-checks is a reasonable means of working to improve the quality of message as it moves from sender to receiver. Talking to the senders about feedback and receivers about the messages is a first step toward identifying potential gaps.

## Common Communications Problems and the Communications Model

Knowing the components of the communications model is critical if the project manager must identify where a communications breakdown is occurring. Sometimes the breakdown occurs in the message. Sometimes, the concerns surface with the selection of media, and sometimes it is just noise.

A basic communications model includes a sender, a receiver, and a message (as shown in Figure 1.1). The message is transmitted through a medium (voice, written word, radio, television, instant message, Web page, and so on) after being encoded by the sender. As it travels through that medium, a variety of filters are applied (including language, understanding, physical distance, and so on) that alter the message as it arrives for decoding by the receiver. As the message is received, other distractions, or noise, may interfere, ranging from a ringing cell phone to a window washer dangling outside the window. The message is received and decoded and may prompt some feedback to the sender in a variety of different forms. Each of these components in the communications model represents both opportunity and risk: opportunity to enhance the understanding; and risk of losing the message.

The *sender* is the individual or group responsible for issuing the initial message. The sender's responsibility is to "consciously construct" [6] the information she wishes to convey. The *message* is the body of information the sender is attempting to communicate. As the sender builds the message, he or she has the opportunity to develop an idea into a comprehensive whole and to share information with clarity. He or she also risks providing information that is unnecessary, extraneous, or superfluous and losing the receiver in a sea of data.

The choice of *medium* is crucial in a communications model. As Marshall McLuhan emphasized in his classic work, *Understanding Media: The Extensions of Man* [7], "the medium is the message." Firing a team member via e-mail is considered a violation of conventional business protocol. Firing a team member over a loudspeaker would be even worse. Firing a team member in a one-on-one conversation, off-site, might be considered reasonable and fair. The message is the same. Only the media change. Selecting media in the communications model is a critical issue, because the media can determine how the information is filtered, decoded, and received.

Media can be categorized in a host of different way. Some are intentionally one-way media (speeches, loudspeakers), while others are intensely intimate (one-on-one, face-to-face communications). Some are remote (e-mail, instant messaging, teleconferences), while others are direct (meetings, presentations). Some are broadcast (television, radio), while others are far more narrow in scope (Web sites). The choice of medium can largely determine how a message is received and decoded.

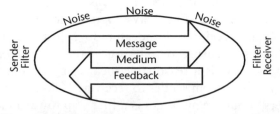

**Figure 1.1**   Model of the communications process.

It is up to the project manager to ascertain which medium is appropriate. If a directive is being issued and no feedback is desired or required, one-way communication may be fitting. If individual, confidential feedback is required, e-mail may be preferred over a team meeting. If the intent is to "wow" the customer or management, a formal presentation may be the correct route. The choice of medium is instrumental in determining how the message is received.

The *receiver* decodes the message through a series of filters. The most common filter is language. Technical jargon can obscure an otherwise crystal-clear message. Acronyms may leave the listener or reader awash in an ocean of misunderstanding. When *en*coding the message, the sender should be mindful of the receiver's ability to *de*code it. Filters are somewhat exclusive to an individual or audience. Noise is not. Noise is any environmental distraction that may detract from the receiver's understanding of the message. The smell of popcorn in the next room may be enough to shut down receipt of a message. A butterfly outside a window can be "noisy" enough to visually distract everyone in a meeting. A cold draft on the back of the neck creates a tactile noise that cannot be ignored.

Once the message is received and decoded, the receiver may provide feedback. Such feedback may be spoken, written, or conveyed through body language or attitude. As the feedback is provided, it becomes a message, and the cycle begins anew.

Communications problems occur when the model breaks down. These concerns manifest themselves in compelling ways. They become evident as problems with project communications. Examples include the following:

- Sender/Receiver Problems
  - Sender fails to send the message. (*The project manager believed he or she sent an e-mail, but it was never sent.*)
  - Receiver fails to receive the message. (*The customer's e-mail system was down for maintenance when the message was sent.*)
  - The message is received in a format that is not understood. (*The message came with an attachment that was in an unfamiliar format.*)
  - The message is received, but misinterpreted. (*The project manager used the term network to refer to a scheduling diagram, but the customer believed they were discussing computer systems.*)
  - The message is sent, but the sender is unavailable. (*The customer is on a weeklong holiday.*)
- Message Problems
  - The message is incomplete. (*Only the first seven chapters of an eight-chapter book are transmitted.*)
  - The message is sent to the wrong party. (*The project manager delivers a message to his or her subcontractor to the customer by accident.*)
  - The message is in the wrong language. (*A project team member delivers an explanation to the customer using extensive technical jargon.*)
- Medium Problems
  - The wrong medium is chosen. (*The project manager sends a sensitive message about the customer relationship via e-mail.*)

- The medium is misused. (*The project manager leaves a 20-minute voice-mail.*)
- The medium is broken. (*The e-mail system transcribes the message into unintelligible jargon.*)

Most, if not all, of these problems have common solutions. Those common solutions are rooted in the notion that the more consistency that is applied to communications, the more readily the messages can be sent and received and the more likely they are to be understood. If status reports take on the same format week after week after week, team members know how to fill them out properly and can more quickly and efficiently update their status on the project. When the customers receive those reports, they know where to look for the information they consider germane because they have seen the reports before and are accustomed to seeking out the information they want. If a project manager knows that a team member always leaves voice-mails that are 30 seconds in length or less, those messages are more likely to be well received than if the messages vary from a few seconds to many-minutes-long diatribes. Consistency is the key.

The project manager seeking effective communication seeks some measure of consistency. The project manager must ensure that the messages are sent and received and that they are clearly understood by all parties involved. The way to ensure that actually happens is to use common approaches, forms, templates, and structures that clearly communicate what the receiver needs to know and when the receiver needs to know it.

## Selecting the Right Tools

The remainder of this book is made up of tools, templates, and structures designed to afford that level of clarity. No project manager should use all of the tools in this book. They should be chosen for their propriety to the project environment, the customer, and the team. In determining if a tool, template, or approach is correct for the project, the project manager should ask these questions:

- Does this tool serve my particular purpose?
- Can it be applied in my environment?
- Is the content of the tool readily available in my environment?
- Am I adept at working with this type of approach?
- Are there other considerations that make this particularly effective in my organizational culture?

If the answer is "yes" to all of those questions, then the tool may be appropriate for the project, the project manager, and the team.

Communications requirements are largely driven by the selection of tools and technologies that are going to be applied, and the selections of those are driven by stakeholder needs. Nonetheless, some requirements are consistent for all projects. For quality communications, protocols for communication must be established, sender/receiver responsibilities need to be identified, data repositories need to be established, and change procedures for these practices have to be in place.

Establishing protocols is a managerial function at a high level, although implementation may be done by team members. *Protocols* are the steps that must be followed to ensure clear communication. They represent *how* communications are to be done. Anyone who remembers his or her first experience filling out an income tax form (or any detailed government form) remembers the challenges. Information is requested that cannot be found. Forms or attachments are identified that are unavailable. Blanks on the form refer to other blanks or other forms, and the information *there* is blank. Out of frustration, many people call in professionals to help fill out the forms. Those professionals know the process. They know what to ask for and how to gather it and where the information is available. For each form and procedure included in this book, specific steps are given on how and where to gather the data. Those are *procedures*. They become protocols when they are mandated by the manager or the organization. The more the project manager can do to ensure the protocols are supported and enabled, the more consistent the communication will become.

As a component of institutionalizing communication, sender and receiver responsibilities must be identified. In a casual conversation, the sender and receiver have very little responsibility. They convey information and respond. They may identify shortcomings in the message or misinterpretation because of noise or filters, but their responsibilities are between themselves. No one else necessarily cares about or needs to be privy to the insights. In a larger environment, responsibilities become more significant. Senders need to be aware of contractual obligations for communication, customer promises, and organizational mandates. Receivers need to capture their concerns in such a fashion that those concerns may be addressed. Their role may be to simply provide feedback (e.g., "message received and understood"), or it may be to provide specific responses within designated time frames. Those roles need to be established for each critical stakeholder so that he or she is aware of and concurs with his or her communications responsibilities.

Once responsibilities are established, the communicators can move forward and determine the appropriate media and tools (the focus of this text).

## References

[1]   Acker, D. D., *Skill in Communication,* Fort Belvoir, VA: Defense Systems Management College, 1992.

[2]   Vaughan, D., *The Challenger Launch Decision,* Chicago, IL: University of Chicago Press, 1996.

[3]   Grunwald, M., "A Tower of Courage," *Washington Post,* Style Section, October 28, 2001.

[4]   Pritchard, C., and L. Ward, *Conversations on Passing the PMP® Exam,* 2nd ed., Arlington, VA: ESI International, 2001.

[5]   "Salt Lake Organizing Committee Selected as 2003 Project of the Year by Project Management Institute," Press Release, Newton Square, PA: Project Management Institute, September 2003.

[6]   Nikander, I. O., *Early Warnings: A Phenomenon in Project Management,* Espoo, Finland: Helsinki University of Technology, 2002.

[7]   McLuhan, M., *Understanding Media: The Extensions of Man,* New York: Signet Books, 1964.

## CHAPTER 2

# Project Communications Technology and Media

Although the focus of this book is specific tools that support project communication, the media that support those tools are critical. In a handful of years, the modes and capabilities of the information storage and transfer media will have doubled or tripled in type, speed, and capacity—that is the nature of modern communications. The greatest evidence of this informational assault can be found in computer-based technologies, but that does not mean that more conventional technologies and approaches are moot. The technologies and media examined here include computer-based, audio, video, traditional written, and verbal communications.

Chapters 3 through 7 will thoroughly examine the nature of a variety of tools and templates that could be applied using many of the technologies and approaches presented in this chapter. Stakeholder analyses, for example, can be captured in the project management software or in forms, presentations, or e-mail. The tools and templates are not generally exclusive to a single medium. This discussion focuses on the media that are at the project manager's disposal and how they are best applied.

## Computer-Based Technology

### Project Management Software

Project managers often speak a language all their own. That language has been reflected in a special class of software since shortly after the advent of computers. Project management software was developed to track activities and tasks, to facilitate understanding of the project, and to find a way to communicate that understanding to others. Project management software packages (e.g., Microsoft Project, Sciforma Project Schedule, Niku Workbench, Planview, Primavera, Artemis Prestige, and so on) have the ability to produce project reports. Although those reports take on wildly different appearances, they share common data sets regarding project work, resource allocation, precedence relationships, and cost and tracking information. They share the ability to present information in a spreadsheet format or in a series of reports. They share the capacity to modify the presentation (to varying degrees) to facilitate understanding.

The tools are not, however, common desktop applications outside the project management community. Also, although most project managers have a copy of one project management program or another on their desktop, they cannot expect their peers who are *not* project managers to have the same tools. Thus, from a communications perspective, the information from project management software needs to be transferable to other tools and applications, including spreadsheet and word processing programs. For many project managers, the most critical component of a project management software package is not the robustness of its algorithms, but the tool's capacity to have outputs copied into a spreadsheet.

In selecting project management software, the project manager should take the tool's exporting ability into account as a mission-critical capability. Tools that severely limit what information can be transferred out and how that information can be transferred will limit the ability to communicate.

## E-Mail

One place where project information must often ultimately be transferred is into an e-mail. E-mail is another vital application for project managers, because it allows for the asynchronous transfer of information from the project team to others inside or outside the team, either en masse or singly. The ubiquity of e-mail and its widespread acceptance places it among (if not the) dominant media for project communications. E-mail is a powerful medium, but it is not without problems, the least of which is the virtual sea of detritus downloaded in the form of mass advertising, which can sometimes drown out the important messages.

E-mail protocols should be carefully outlined in the project communications plan (Chapter 4) to ensure that project messages are elevated to visibility and to ensure that project team members have a consistent vision as to what information is appropriately transferred (and, as a result, maintained) by this medium and what information is not. Considerations that should be outlined in the project communications plan relating to e-mail include the following:

- Appropriate/inappropriate language and/or areas of discussion;
- Subject line protocols and practices;
- Carbon-copy and "blind" carbon-copy practices (for both the initial "send" as well as the reply);
- Document retention procedures.

If not effectively controlled, e-mail can become a weak communications medium, not because of a lack of use, but because of misuse and misunderstanding of the tool.

## Project Web Sites

Most organizations of any size already have an Internet-based Web site. And even for the handful that do not, the investment in a project Web site is sufficiently nominal that it is within the financial reach of most projects. Project Web sites may range in style, use, and application from a graphics-intensive bulletin board rich with project information to a simple "closet" housing project data. In either instance, some commonalities will afford effective use of the Internet as a project tool.

The first challenge with project Web sites is accessibility with security. If a project Web site is left open to the public, team members are guaranteed the ability to tap into the site and its information at will. If a project Web site is left open to the public, however, almost anyone will be able to find their way to the information and apply it for their own purposes. Data security becomes a major issue. Even Web sites with password access and higher levels of security can be hacked, which limits the willingness of some organizations to post information in such a public forum. Multiple levels of security (Web site access passwords and individual document passwords) can improve the sense of confidence, but are still not infallible in their ability to protect an organization's secrets. Many organizations' "secrets," however, are not really of interest to outside organizations and may be posted, preserved, and shared on the Internet with reasonable impunity.

Because some security measures will almost invariably be used, the project manager's responsibility for a project Web site is to ensure that team members are updated on how to access the site and on what information they may expect to find there. A Web site with excessive security is a library with a locked door. The information is there, but no one can have access to it, and team members will only try the "door" a limited number of times before finding alternative means to access the information they desire or require.

The other critical notion with any project Web site is the currency of information. Information maintained on a project Web site must actually be kept up to date. If the Internet site becomes a repository for outdated information without being refreshed, the site will rapidly fall into disuse. The project manager and his or her archivist should establish protocols for information shared on the Web site, including when it will be updated, formats that will be used, how frequently security access will be modified, and how team members working to reach the site can get outside assistance. Because help desk support for internal Web sites is generally limited, the support and assistance is normally established within the team.

## Web-Based Communications

A project Web site is not the only Web application used in project management. Instant messaging and real-time chat room capabilities have changed the way in which meetings are held. In some organizations, employees are required to have their desktops enabled with one of the popular instant messaging systems (e.g., AOL Instant Messenger and Windows Messenger) so that even if the team is distributed around the globe, team members can instantly "stop down the hall" to share information any time a team member is at her terminal. Such Web-based chat capabilities are common in nonbusiness applications, but their use in corporate communication is becoming progressively more common.

The only hurdle to true corporate ubiquity is the concern over the potential for security breaches caused by instant messaging systems. This has prompted some organizations to create their own internal messaging systems, which have the advantage of high levels of security, but lack the capacity to share information outside the organization.

Although the use of such information exchanges can greatly enhance communications speed, they can also cause information overload. Some users cannot manage the onslaught of information associated with multiple messages arriving from multiple users on their computer desktop while they are trying to work on something else. As with the other types of Internet communication, the protocols to determine how on-line messaging should be used need to be incorporated within the communications plan.

### Personal Digital Assistants

Many project managers now carry *personal digital assistants* (PDAs) to monitor and track their day-to-day activities. Many of these PDAs now have embedded wireless communications technology, which means that they wed some of the most advantageous aspects of both synchronous and asynchronous communications. PDAs provide the advantage of having a computer connection with the office when the project manager is in the field, without the bulk of a laptop.

In using the PDA for inbound communication, the project manager should make clear to team members and those with direct access to the PDA connection that large attachments and significant graphics should be kept to a minimum. It is sometimes easy for the sender to believe that the PDA is nothing more than a computer in miniature, but PDAs generally do have some significant limitations in terms of large-scale memory and video display capability.

For outbound communication, the greatest limitation of PDAs as a communications technology is frequently that there is no simple user interface to input data into the tool. Although stylized alphabets have been created to expedite stylus writing on PDA pads, the ability to input is generally much slower than is available through touch typing. And while some PDAs have keyboard attachments, those attachments are sometimes unwieldy for day-to-day, in-the-field applications. This limitation makes large documents difficult to generate and may also inhibit the user's ability to format the information being sent (particularly in spreadsheet or word processing applications).

## Audio Technologies

### Teleconferencing

Telephone conferences are a commonplace business tool, but the depth and variety of approaches have changed in recent years. A number of years ago, having more than four or five individuals on a teleconference would have been considered unwieldy. Now, technology affords the ability to include hundreds or even thousands of persons on a single conference call. Such large-scale teleconferences are frequently Internet supported, featuring an on-line presentation, coupled with a discussion led by a handful of individuals on the virtual teleconference "stage." Participants can raise questions through the Internet interface, but the discussion can still be dominated by those in charge.

The conventional teleconference of a few key players is still commonplace as well. In all of these scenarios, the key to successful implementation is knowing when it is appropriate for the parties to speak and how they have to manage the mechanics of the call. Perhaps the most challenging aspect of teleconferencing for many people is that they forget the common courtesy of regular personal identification (e.g., "This is Roger again, and I think..."). Because of the distortion inherent in many ordinary telephone receivers, frequent personal identification is essential to maintain a clear flow of information.

Even when the technical challenges are overcome, the teleconference has the inherent difficulty of lacking face-to-face contact (as do most remote technologies). As such, parties in the conference should ask for clarification any time there are any misgivings about what is being said. The content of a conference call should be clearly outlined at the beginning of the call and should be identified with clear objectives for each content element. If the content requires support documentation, such documentation should be sent (via fax, e-mail, or posted mail) prior to the call, and there should be premeeting affirmation that the support documentation has been received. The call should be treated as a meeting, with a clear agenda, and with all conversation directed at the agenda. Because conference calls can get confusing in terms of who is speaking and any references they may make, any time the agenda is amended or superseded, there should be a clear definition of the objective of the new subject matter discussion.

Clear rules of behavior should be established regarding when it is appropriate to speak, interrupt, or join the conversation. It is also important to establish basic protocols for such simple things as putting the conference on "hold" (where "hold" music may become a distraction), putting the phone on mute (without which participants' background noise may grow intolerable), or identifying oneself at the beginning of each speaking "turn." If some participants are there simply to listen, it may be necessary at intervals throughout the call to affirm their presence or ongoing participation through a call of the roll or a simple check on status (e.g., "Bob? Are you still with us?").

Conference calls can become a major distraction, because participants have the potential to stray from topic (as any meeting does). Conference calls can cause frustration if participants misinterpret tone of voice during the conversation. Discussion should be measured and even, and speakers should make an effort to minimize intense, rapid speech. Without the context of body language and facial expressions to support the language, it can readily be misinterpreted. As such, any time a conference call is perceived as *causing* misunderstanding, the topic at hand should be set aside long enough to clarify the emotional context of the participants and their understanding of what is being said.

## Voice-Mail

For some, voice-mail is the technology of choice for project management. As with e-mail, it allows for asynchronous communication and opens the door to transfer information at whim or will. As with e-mail, however, it also has a downside in that some individuals use it inappropriately or to excess. Voice-mail is most effective (as with virtually all communication) when there are clear procedures be followed as ritual. Limiting durations, clarifying contact information, and providing information succinctly can all make the voice-mail experience far more positive. Failure to establish such guidelines can lead to inconsistency and misunderstanding.

## Telephone Calls

Conventional telephone calls are intended for the quick transfer of information with some measure of immediacy. They may also be used for clarification of issues that were not transmitted effectively in written or graphic form. They are used liberally in modern business, but should be limited to those situations where an extensive documentary record is not essential or where time is of the essence. They may also be used appropriately when the sender is not effective at sharing information via the written word.

The nature of telephone conversations should be brief and clarifying. Attempting a long-form review of any project element of significance during a phone call invites the opportunity for disagreements and misunderstandings about what was said or how the information was conveyed. The classic "he-said/she-said" types of arguments can be driven by poorly chosen content for such discussions.

On the telephone, particularly in one-on-one conversations, the lack of body language leaves voice alone to carry the message. For some senders, voice quality is not an issue. For others, a monotone quality to their voice may be normal, but may be construed as being bored. Rapid-fire speech may be interpreted as aggressive, and overly slow speech may simply frustrate the receiver. The approach should be one of conversational tone, coupled with a willingness to be patient and listen to the responses thoroughly before providing feedback.

If the call is intended to be a component of the official project record, it should be followed by an affirming e-mail, memo, or telephone log entry (Chapter 5). A phone log, if kept, is nothing more than a sequential record of times, dates, callers, and nature of the calls.

Perhaps the most significant modern considerations come with the use of a cellular phone. The microphones on such telephones are extremely sensitive, and yet some users feel compelled to speak loudly into them because of the devices' size and weight. Due to improvements in cellular technology, such phones frequently have higher quality and better microphone sensitivity than a wired unit and should be treated in the same fashion (with a reasonable level of privacy required).

## Video Technologies

### Videoconferencing

Many organizations have sufficient bandwidth to conduct videoconferences over the Internet, and some that have not yet reached that point have access via direct lines with videoconferencing centers in other cities or other facilities. The videoconference should be used when (because of graphics, presentation content, or physical disability) a teleconference would be insufficient to meet the need.

Videoconferences generally require a higher level of rehearsal and testing than other communications tools, because the technology is relatively unfamiliar to most users. Videoconferences are normally limited to one or two remote sites because of the few seconds of lag time involved in getting information from one site to the other. Although that may seem an inconsequential period of time, those seconds make the difference between normal conversation across a conference table and a stilted conversation with accidental overlaps and miscues.

Those awkward moments can be overcome through planning and coordination. The key in videoconferences is to identify gestures, cues, or handoffs that will facilitate more ordinary conversation. The other key is to encourage those who are not familiar to avoid some of the most common missteps or miscues of applying the technology. A classic example is the propensity for some videoconference users to stare at the television screen, rather than occasionally glance at the camera (if it is not properly placed adjacent to the receiving television screen). It causes the viewers on the "other end" to perceive that the focus of the discussion is elsewhere. The camera is the "eye" of the receiver, and a failure to look the other participants in the eyes can interfere with basic communication.

There is a need in videoconferences to limit some of the presentation graphic support material. Because some remote screens may be as small as 15 inches, highly detailed graphics may not be effectively supported. Otherwise, the content may be virtually the same as any other meeting.

Videoconferences are most frequently beset by their own technology. Even in organizations with dedicated videoconference rooms, the technology is often sufficiently daunting that full-time technical support becomes essential. That can sometimes limit the efficacy of such presentations.

Also, as with any remote transmission, time zones may become a consideration. A 4:00 p.m. presentation on the East coast of the United States will be happening at 9:00 p.m. in the United Kingdom, and at 6:00 a.m. in the Pacific Rim. The needs of the remote participants need to be taken into account in the videoconference environment.

## Remote Presentations

Remote presentations take the videoconference to the next level. Remote presentations are presentations in which the receivers cannot actively participate, so the sender speaks to a large audience via technology similar to that applied in a videoconference. The difference is that because of the larger audience size and because the presentation is purely outbound, the focus on the sender is all the more intense. Concerns such as audience focus, proper language, decorum, and idiomatic language are amplified for the one presenter because nobody else is participating in the process. Success in the remote presentation environment is rooted in the same principles as success in the videoconference environment. Preparation and a thorough understanding of the audience, the technology, and the environment are essential to success.

In building a presentation for remote delivery, the content should be direct, clear, and unambiguous. Complex ideas should be rendered as less complex analogies that the audience can see or hear and readily understand. The content should be rendered in digestible segments, because one-way communication does not encourage active listening and participation. In video presentations, the graphics should be simple, because the presentation screens being used by the receivers may be as small as DVD playback units, which do not allow for a great deal of detail. (Granted, most remote presentations are projected on larger screens, but there is no guarantee of how the content will be used *and reused*.)

As with any presentation, the content should express the clear intent of the presentation at the outset, deliver that intent, and then affirm that the intent has been met. In dealing with remote media, presenters frequently forget the basics. Microphones do not require the presenter to use a louder voice. Cameras are the eyes of the audience, rather than monitors. In video production, the most common problem is a failure to look directly into the lens of the camera, as though it were the eyes of the audience. Because, for the presenter, the "audience" frequently consists of little more than a cameraman and a sound engineer, there is sometimes a temptation to present to those individuals. A warm relationship with the camera lens will convey the message more effectively.

Remote presentations do have their advantages. They allow the presentation or discussion to be reused, and they enable presentations in venues where temporal or physical constraints would normally render them impossible. Still, true communication is a two-way street, and the remote presentation is a one-way avenue.

### Video/Snapshot Phone

In just the past few years, a cellular technology has taken hold like few others, that of the snapshot phone. Although such a novelty might seem inappropriate for business applications, nothing could be further from the truth. From validating the look and feel of potential deliverables to ensuring you can identify the person with whom you are dealing, the cell phones with built-in cameras and transmission protocols create the distinct advantage of generating a new opportunity to build clearer relationships and better understanding with peers on the other end.

While the pictures are small and do not afford any significant quality in resolution, they can be helpful in broader applications. Still, the same issues as exist with videoconferencing (proper use, focus, and decorum) need to be kept in mind in this much smaller-scale application.

## Traditional Written Communications Media

### Reports

The word *report* has its roots in Latin, meaning "to carry back." Reports are designed to carry back an account of what has happened, and may range from a simple paragraph on project activity to a multivolume analysis of how the project evolved and an interpretation of that information. This book is replete with reports of various types. The common thread that they should share is that their objective is to carry back accurate information about what has transpired.

The key consideration in building reports should be the reader's ability to assimilate the information provided in the report and the conformity of the report with accepted practice either within the organization or within the industry. Many government reports, for example, must follow specific formats. That level of consistency affords regular readers the ability to cull the information they seek in relatively short order. The information is easier to access because the formats are familiar.

Reports should make a clear distinction between the reporting of fact and the interpretation of those facts into opinion or conclusions. Many reports will have separate headings or chapters to more clearly make the distinction between the two. That division is important because it has the potential to allow readers to distinguish when they do not concur with the conclusions and when they do not concur with the facts. That can simplify any later discussion on concerns associated with the report, allowing one element or the other to stand.

Reports may be simple (or extended) narratives, or in some cases, may be retained in specific forms.

### Forms

Many organizations will establish forms to allow for consistent reporting of information without a lot of interpretation. Forms encourage consistent reporting and ensure consistent inclusion of specific data elements. Many of the communications tools included in this book are forms. Forms serve as a powerful means to reinforce what is important in a document and what is not. They limit the inclusion of extraneous data and generate conformity.

In process-driven organizations, forms are seen as an essential element of success. Because processes are frequently subject to interpretation, forms limit the amount of interpretation and latitude in the communications process. In some environments, forms are a welcome addition, because they stem the amount of time and energy that has to be invested in developing formats for communication and determining which informational elements are critical and which are not. On the other hand, forms often generate some enmity, in that they frequently inhibit creativity and stifle the information that can be presented.

Good forms will consist of both the form *and* some guidance as to how the form is properly applied, reviewed, and maintained.

### Planners

For some project managers, the primary form of communication is a very personal one—their daily planner. These paper-based and/or computerized planners (generated by a variety of different organizations such as Day-Timer and Franklin-Covey) capture the detailed daily activities of the owner. In some instances, however, they are used beyond simple tracking of meetings and gatherings. The documents and binders sometimes serve as the scheduling and communications link between their owners and the outside world. Some managers allow access to their planners (or the software that supports them) to assign meeting times, plan for gatherings, or to set up one-on-one conversations. Others use the binder as a means to flag important events that either have happened or are pending.

For those who use their planners religiously, their planners themselves can become their favorite form of communication. For those who do not use them, they may be perceived as administrative overhead without a great deal of additional value. Before dismissing their use, however, it is wise to determine if any of the key participants in the process are active users.

## Traditional Verbal Communications Media

Most of the other media discussed up to this point have been the type that can be captured in documents, paper, and virtual forms. The remaining media are verbally oriented, but are frequently supported by paper tools (as project status meetings are supported by the project status report). This section focuses on the oral aspects of the media, rather than the documentation that supports it. For all of these, some form of postdiscussion documentation can be appropriate.

### Ad Hoc Conversations

The most common verbal communications medium is the traditional conversation. It is often suggested that more project communication goes on at the coffee machine than is ever conducted in meetings. Ad hoc conversations facilitate the social and business interactions that make projects possible. They are often the foundation on which much of the project is built. Their purpose is to fill in the gaps of understanding left by other media and to affirm a common understanding of all aspects of the project environment.

Such conversations are used whenever and wherever two project stakeholders meet, and they are used to clarify project information as well as individual interpretations of that information. In many instances, the clarity derived from a casual conversation in the hall provides more depth than can be generated in the *work breakdown structure*. Because these conversations are not planned, however, they should not be relied on as a key supplement to other project planning or clarification tools.

Again, because these conversations are not planned, their content cannot inherently be preordained. For the project manager and project team, however, some limitations should be established on the content of such conversations. Whenever the conversations stray into commitments to a customer, reallocation of resources, modification of contractual arrangements, or anything requiring formal approval, the conversation should be redirected to a more formal setting (such as a meeting). Other limitations (such as limitations on the nature of conversations about other project stakeholders) may be ordained by the project team, but may be far more difficult to enforce. By directing project team members (as soon as they join the project team) on the propriety of certain ad hoc conversations, it becomes easier to affirm other processes that encourage extensive documentation and tracking of any project commitments. Although ad hoc conversations should be encouraged, they cannot become the final word on any long-term project commitment or approach.

These conversations can make or break a project, depending on their tone, team member attitudes toward the project, and the types of information that are exchanged. Although they cannot be directly controlled, they should be addressed by the project manager early in the project to establish the appropriate tone for such conversations, particularly when external stakeholders are involved.

### Meetings

Many projects seem to revolve around the notion that meetings are the primary communications medium, and all vital communications will take place in meetings. Although that statement is not generally true, the perception is one that ties in with the notion that meetings may determine how the project and the project team are perceived within their own organization, the customer organization, and among other stakeholders.

Meetings are intended as data-gathering, data-sharing, and data-organization sessions. They are intended to generate not only shared understanding, but also a general sense of direction. Meetings are held any time there is a need to achieve consensus on information and its interpretation. They should be used when a unified vision on how to approach the project or a project issue is critical (in contrast to situations in which a single individual's vision or approach will drive the issue). They may be used to generate understanding or when there is a need to mutually participate in development of deliverables.

The objectives of any meeting should be clearly defined. It is important to delineate the specific deliverables and artifacts that will be generated by the end of the meeting, in order to focus effort toward those artifacts. Sample agenda for various types of meetings are given in Chapters 4 through 7.

The approaches to working in such a group setting are widely varied. Most will involve significant team coordination and facilitation skills. The facilitation should involve a reiteration of the meeting deliverable(s) and the identification of those individuals present in the meeting who can directly contribute. The key role of the facilitator is to ensure that the agenda are covered thoroughly and that all of the issues the meeting was to address are addressed.

The project manager may take on a variety of roles in this setting. The project manager may be called on to serve as facilitator, minute-taker, and participant. Regardless of the project manager's effectiveness, no one can serve in all of those roles without diminishing at least one of them. That is why the project managers may want to hire professionals to serve in the roles that they do not see as part of their strengths. Professional facilitators or archivists can keep the meeting moving forward, allowing the project manager to focus on the project and the concerns it raises.

Also, if the meeting includes an extensive body of remote participants, certain types of activities may prove impossible without the use of virtual whiteboards or other Internet-supported interactive displays. If the meeting will include development of any extensive graphic artifacts, the participation modes to be used by remote participants should be considered before the meeting begins.

Meetings may last a matter of hours or days. The determination about duration should reflect the meeting deliverables' size and complexity. If the meeting is to produce specific outputs for customer consumption, it may be worth several days of participants' time. If it is to produce an understanding of who is to work on particular components of the project, 30 minutes may be sufficient.

In some organizations, meeting attendance is seen as a badge of honor. Thus, meeting invitations may become politically charged, because some representatives will want to be invited simply to affirm their political standing in the organization(s). Clear criteria should be established regarding who should attend specific meetings, which allows for an unambiguous rationale for the attendees list.

As a meeting progresses, documentation should be developed. Once the meeting ends, that documentation should be edited for clarity and disseminated to all participants for their records.

## Presentations

Presentations are opportunities to share information with a broad audience. They are often used to sell a perspective or to engender greater levels of support. Presentations are designed to persuade. Presentations can be used to communicate intent or actions "up" the organization to higher echelons of management. They can be used to provide information to peer levels within the organization or to provide training and/or direction to team members, end users, or virtually any audience.

Presentations should have a specific focus or intent, and that intent should be clearly expressed to the audience at the beginning of the presentation. The audience should also be given a clear sense of the agenda for the presentation and the schedule. Those elements allow the audience members to track their progress through the presentation experience. Presentation content and tone should be respectful, acknowledging the participants and their commitment of time to the presentation. If data are presented using presentation software (e.g., PowerPoint or Freelance), the information should be kept to a reasonable level on each slide. If there is more information than can reasonably be presented through the presentation software, handouts should be used to augment the presentation. Presentation software is a generally accepted standard for presentations, but is by no means required. Some presentations can be conducted without such support. If presentation software is used, the presenter should be *extremely* careful not to simple read the slides verbatim. While the slides may provide guidance and direction for the project presentation, they should augment the verbal presentation, rather than mirror it. Presentations are well received when they provide information clearly and memorably.

## Press Briefings

Few environments are as grueling for a project manager as when he or she must face the media. Press briefings are held to inform members of the media about the status of a project, its environment, or its supporting organization. They are intended to present the project organization (or host organization) in the best possible light. Press briefings are held when a project or its impact is sufficiently significant that public information campaigns using mass media are appropriate. They should be held whenever the project has achieved sufficient recognition that the project organization's perspective on the effort is deemed to be of public interest. That recognition may be positive or negative in nature, and may be proactive or reactive, depending on the nature of the project organization.

The subject matter for a press briefing should be determined well in advance of the briefing to ensure that the correct information is shared and any information that the organization does *not* want to share is clearly defined for those hosting the briefing. Members of the media are often given "press kits" at such gatherings (Chapter 3), highlighting corporate history, general information, past press releases, and any contact persons' business cards. The organizational spokesperson (sometimes, the project manager) should open with a statement regarding the nature of the project and the issue(s) that brought the project into the public eye. The statement should anticipate any questions, objections, or concerns that may be raised. If broadcast media are present, consideration should be given to phrases, paragraphs, or references that may be presented in 8- to 20-second sections (classic "sound bites").

A press briefing need not necessarily include question-and-answer periods, but keep in mind that most members of the media will have questions. Although the spokesperson is not compelled to answer these questions, failure to respond is sometimes interpreted as a lack of cooperation or as a sign of deviousness. In situations where off-the-cuff responses may be dangerous, it is wholly appropriate to offer to do supplemental research and respond at a later time. The most effective spokespersons will identify the time when the additional information will be available and how it will be made available. If "no comment" is the appropriate response, alternative means to couch that phrase can be very effective and can leave media representatives with something quotable. Saying "This would not be the time to offer comment on something of that nature," followed by an iteration of the key point of the briefing affords the presenter the opportunity to emphasize what *is* important.

Press briefings are potentially volatile situations, but they are the host organization's to control. Simple considerations (like morning coffee and comfortable seating arrangements) can go a long way to defuse a potentially hostile audience. Clear rules of conduct and engagement can also minimize the possibility that the session appears to be out of control—and the more that can be done to ensure a positive attitude and a forward-looking perspective, the better.

## Other Media

Other media, from smoke signals to semaphores, could also be considered in the project context. For the sake of this text, however, the media selected are those that are in most common use. The remainder of this text focuses on how to convey information within these media, acknowledging that some tools will serve better as traditional forms, while others support meetings, presentations, or videoconferences. The effective project communicator will be sufficiently astute to know which media she prefers and which tend to be more challenging. By wedding these media to the proper tools for the situation, the project manager can take a significant step toward more effective communication.

## Conclusion

The tools outlined in the remainder of this book will be communicated using a relatively consistent format. First, they are subdivided by the project *process* in which they are applied. In reality, virtually all communications tools, ideally, would be developed, evaluated, and approved very early in the project life cycle, but their ideal application often comes later in the project. So these tools are arranged by the processes they ultimately serve and in simple alphabetical order within those processes. For each tool, the text strives to identify the purposes for which the tool is developed, how the tool is applied in the project environment, the content of the tool itself, the various approaches that may be applied in its use, and any special considerations that might be worthwhile in using the tool.

## CHAPTER 3

# Communication Tools in the Initiating Processes

Many communications tools are introduced early in a project's life. That's because the need for communications is at its highest when a project is new. By sheer volume, the tools may overwhelm some first-time users. Although setting expectations early in the project is important, it is equally important not to inundate the uninitiated with too much data. Consider the purpose of the communications tool before applying it. In many instances, it may not *have* to be introduced early in the project. In other cases, advising the other parties in the process that they will be responsible for certain types of communication is essential from the very outset.

All of these tools ultimately serve (in one way or another) as a component of the communications plan. They serve either as a subcomponent of the plan itself, or as an adjunct to the plan, complementing its intent. Although the details of building a communications plan are not discussed until later in the book, the rationale for communications planning should already be obvious. If there is no structure for integrating existing stakeholders in the informational "loop," then communications and information transfer will eventually break down. Even in the best relationships, there are communications hurdles to be overcome. Ill-timed, poorly thought out communication can fracture even the hardiest of associations. These tools are designed to afford some consistency to the communications processes.

Also, each tool discussed in this book may have *some* application in virtually any phase of the project. Because project phases vary widely from organization to organization, the remainder of this text is arranged according to the processes in which the tool is applied. The tools in this chapter focus on the initiating process. According to the Project Management Institute's *Guide to the Project Management Body of Knowledge,* initiating processes are those associated with authorizing the project or phase [1].

## Approvals

### Purpose

Project approvals are those signatures required to achieve authorization of phases, milestones, resource allocation, or virtually any aspect of the project that requires acceptance or authorization by another party. Projects may be subject to dozens of approval cycles throughout their lifetimes. The communications aspect of approvals is to ensure that they are shared, understood, and spread consistently within the organization. The basic purpose of approvals is to validate and provide acceptance of a project.

## Application

Approvals are normally conducted in writing and represent a commitment on the part of stakeholders. To receive an approval, the basic premise for which approval is sought must be documented thoroughly and clearly. This may be done through an approvals template, checklist, or other means, but normally requires a signature. Approvals can take a host of different forms, but those that are most effective will include a succinct statement of what is being approved and a clear representation of the authority of the individual(s) approving it, such as a signature. For example, an approval may be a simple acknowledgment that a milestone has been achieved:

> The current status of the project, as defined in the status report dated March 1, is acceptable, and performance to date has been up to expectations.
> X   Megan DeBills, Customer

The approvals can then be archived, displayed, or channeled out to team members for their awareness.

## Content

Approvals should always include a statement of what is being approved and the depth or range of the approval. Approvals represent closure of a sales experience, even when nothing is being sold or exchanged. The exchange of value with an approval is frequently one of basic progress and forward momentum on the project.

## Approaches

While approvals may be given verbally, written approvals are perceived as inherently carrying more weight and value. Even if the approvals are for issues of a seemingly minor nature, requesting signatures serves the dual function of affirming that the other stakeholder is aware of what she is approving and that the approval has significance and meaning. Specific action or reaction (e.g., movement to the next phase, initiation of the next deliverable) should be tied to approvals [2].

In the virtual environment, paper signatures may not be possible. That should not preclude the effort to get positive affirmation in any approval process. The most effective means for getting true e-mail approvals is to ask the approving authority to use a specific type of language or verbiage as affirmation. Asking the approving authority to write in response that "This e-mail serves as my authorization and approval of [the approval in question]" serves as a tool to minimize the ambiguity sometimes associated with virtual approvals and authorizations.

Although verbal approvals are among the most commonplace in industry, they carry little long-term weight. To be effective, the manager should seriously consider following up with affirmative documentation (either on paper or via e-mail) as described earlier.

### Considerations

Many organizations promote a culture that is accountability averse, but that does not make accountability, particularly in the project environment, any less desirable. The manager who can introduce accountability into the approvals process (where it has not existed in the past) can find their projects easier to promote, since they alone have the documentation to affirm support of the effort to date. Introducing that accountability early sets the stage for those who join the project later, because it will help them develop an understanding of the expectation for approvals and signatures.

Objectivity should also be a goal in achieving approvals, because approval of a subjective set of criteria may have very limited weight in that one person's interpretation of the criteria may differ wildly from another's.

## Business Case[1]

### Purpose

The business case establishes the fundamental rationale for a course of action. It is the documented history of why a project, effort, or approach was selected. It details the objectives, the projected outcomes, and the projected investments associated with the effort. As such, it allows decision makers to examine the breadth of information currently known about the effort to determine whether or not the project is a good idea in terms of cost, benefit, and organizational objectives. It may include statements about the impacts on existing business practices, resource constraints, and environmental considerations so as to provide a comprehensive understanding of the project. In some instances, risk analysis is a key component. It is the primary document defending the rationale for the project.

### Application

The business case is normally applied early in the project and may be developed by senior management, marketing groups, the project office, or by any group or organization responsible for initiating large-scale activity within the organization. Business cases in mature organizations follow consistent formats to allow managers to review multiple projects in similar contexts.

The business case will list the key proponents of the project, the sponsor, the users or beneficiaries of the project, and any deliverables. At a high level, it will describe the approach to be used and the business justification or rationale for that approach. Normally, that rationale will incorporate some form of cost/benefit analysis, although the types of cost/benefit analyses and their applications vary widely.

A general outline for a business case might look like this:

1.0   Executive Overview
2.0   Project Description
   2.1   Proponent(s)
   2.2   Sponsor(s)

---

1.   See also *Business Justification, Cost Case.*

## Content

The information supporting each of those outline components should be developed as objectively as possible. To achieve that, each element should be reviewed by *at least* one other person. The content may be expanded (or compressed) based on the business needs of the organization conducting the analysis. At a high level each section should contain the specific information discussed in the following subsections.

### 1.0   Executive Overview

The executive overview is a general scope statement identifying the time, cost, and requirements for the project, as well as the business need driving the effort. It should include the names of the project sponsors and project manager, as well as a description of the beneficiaries of the effort. The executive overview should provide a synopsis of the cost/benefit analysis, regardless of whether those costs and/or benefits are tangible or not.

### 2.0   Project Description

The project description should provide more depth on most of the issues raised in the executive overview, including the background, sources, and history for any data provided as rationale for the project or the cost/benefit analysis. This section may include cross-references to other project documentation, including draft plans, product descriptions, and stakeholder analyses or surveys.

### 3.0   Environmental Considerations

The cultural, technical, or physical environment may described here in depth, providing information on the practices and protocols typical within the environment.

### 4.0   Risk Factors/Risks

The risk approach described here may include the means and practices to be employed for risk identification, qualification, quantification, response development, contingency allocation, and risk reassessment. Any initial or significant risks identified in developing the preliminary information (like the cost/benefit analysis) should be identified here as well.

### 5.0   Assumptions

Assumptions are beliefs that are held as true to allow for ongoing planning. In an effort to ensure that they have value, assumptions identified here regarding all aspects of the project (resources, environment, client culture, organizational behavior, and so on) should be validated as practicable.

### Approaches

Business cases in some organizations may be voluminous and detailed. Others span only a page or two. Regardless of the level of depth, they should provide insight into the considerations that were used to determine if there is a valid business reason for moving forward with a project. They should be directed at an internal audience, because they may include information about the internal response to and structure for the customer relationship. The internal audience should, at a minimum, include the project sponsors, the project manager and executive management.

### Considerations

Because the business case may contain sensitive competitive information, it should be disseminated only to those who have achieved a level of trust within the organization. The author of the document should be clearly identified, and contact information for that individual should be included as well. Although the business case is an initiating document, it should be reviewed and revisited on a regular basis to ensure that the cost/benefit analysis and proposal are still being pursued.

# Business Justification[2]

### Purpose

The business justification is similar to the business case, and in some organizations, the two documents are synonymous. For those who discern a difference, it relates to the use of the business justification to compare and contrast one project with another in the organizational portfolio. The business justification goes beyond simply trying to determine if a single project has sufficient benefits to warrant moving forward with it. It pertains instead to ascertaining the relative value of the project in comparison to other projects in the organization in terms of the organization's business strategies.

### Application

The business justification incorporates the strategic rationale for the project, and it may require an organizational model outlining the various strategies and their

---

2.   See also *Business Case, Cost Case.*

relative weight or importance, or it may list or delineate the ongoing efforts within the organization and the relative importance of this effort to one or more others. In addition, it may incorporate the rationale for one approach in comparison or contrast with another.

The outline may be similar to a business case, with only a few variations:

1.0   Executive Overview
2.0   Project Description
   2.1   Proponent(s)
   2.2   Sponsor(s)
   2.3   Users/Beneficiaries
   2.4   Deliverables and Quality Criteria
   2.5   Rationale
   2.6   Cost/Benefit
   2.7   Communications Requirements
3.0   Strategic Alignment
   3.1   Objectives served
   3.2   Metric scoring
   3.3   Portfolio ranking
4.0   Alternatives
   4.1   Alternatives considered
   4.2   Rationale for dismissal
5.0   Assumptions

## Content

For the components that differ from a business case, the informational requirements are different as well.

### 3.0   Strategic Alignment

The strategic alignment is a statement that identifies the strategic alignment of the project to the organization's stated strategic objectives. For organizations without strategic vision statements, such alignment tends to be ambiguous, at best.

*3.1   Objectives Served*   In the ideal, objectives are captured as unambiguous, realistic evidence that organizational goals are being met. This statement should include detail on the level to which those objectives are being served and the manner in which they are being served.

*3.2   Metric Scoring*   If the organization has a metric portfolio model for scoring projects relative to business and strategic goals, this is where that storing would be reflected.

*3.3   Portfolio Ranking*   Through a mathematic, ordinal, or comparative analysis, the project should be identified for its relative position to other projects in the division's or organization's portfolio.

### 4.0   Alternatives

The alternatives considered may be either alternative projects or alternative approaches to the project under review.

*4.1   Alternatives Considered*   This section should provide a general description of the other approaches that were considered to the project and the nature (and possibly ownership) of those approaches.

*4.2   Rationale for Dismissal*   Rather than defending the existing approach, this should be an explanation of how or why the alternatives that were under consideration were formally dismissed.

## Approaches

Given the different cultures, strategies, and organizational objectives, the comparison process to evaluate projects will differ in virtually all organizations. The key in a business justification is to provide a relative sense of the importance of the project to the other projects (and the alternative approaches for *this* project) that may have been considered. In any instance, the document provides a historic perspective of the relative importance of this effort in contrast to other organizational efforts.

## Considerations

Given the potential overlap with the business case, the two documents may merge into one in some organizations. However, for organizations where a detailed financial business case is not required, the business justification may be sufficient independent of the other tool.

# Cost Case[3]

## Purpose

The cost case provides a detailed cost justification for moving forward with the project, highlighting the financials and their supporting data sources. It also incorporates the relative levels of confidence and validity of the information being considered. It is often a component of the business case.

## Application

The cost justification for the project is often considered the single most important component of the business case or it may stand alone. It is used to present information from accounting, marketing, or other internal financial research departments regarding predicted financial performance (for both costs and revenues) in the context of the organizations preferred metrics. Those metrics may include, but are not limited to, the following:

    Internal rate of return;

---

3.   See also *Business Justification, Business Case.*

Return on investment;

Return on assets;

Return on sales;

Payback period;

Present value;

Net present value;

Cost/benefit ratio;

Cash flow analysis;

Discounted cash flow.

The cost case is broken down by the components of the financial metric, and is comprised of a description of the sources of data and the data for that metric. The cost case is used as a defense of the predictions made regarding project performance and as a historic document to validate how well the organization was able to generate accurate estimates.

## Content

The tool's content is specific to the financial metric selected. *Internal rate of return* (IRR), for example, is comprised of a series of predicted project cash inflows and outflows that serve to drive the potential financial return for the project. A cost case using IRR would incorporate all of the components of the IRR analysis, including the spreadsheet, the sources of data for the spreadsheet, and an interpretation thereof. Table 3.1 shows a sample of a cost case for a project that uses an IRR analysis.

*Inflows:*     Description of source of inflow data (e.g., "Inflow data were derived from the marketing surveys conducted during June/July 2008 by J. Zohnd and Sons. Background research is archived at www.corporateintranet.com.").

*Outflows:*     Description of source of outflow data (e.g., "Outflow data were derived from bottom-up cost estimate conducted by Project Manager Tom Gormely October 2008. Stored on the corporate LAN at m:\archive\proposals\estimates\ gormely07.xls.").

*Interpretation/assessment:*     Analysis of information as presented (e.g., "Since the corporate hurdle rate for IRR is 18%, this project should proceed. It should be noted, however that the success of the project is heavily reliant on revenues from

**Table 3.1**   Sample Cost Case for a Project

| *Cost Case for the Project (Using IRR): Descriptive Title of the Project* | | | |
|---|---|---|---|
| *Year* | *Inflows* | *Outflows* | *Net* |
| Current | 0 | 3,000 | −3,000 |
| Year 1 | 1,000 | 4,000 | −3,000 |
| Year 2 | 3,000 | 1,000 | 2,000 |
| Year 3 | 8,000 | 1,000 | 7,000 |
| INTERNAL RATE OF RETURN: | | | 19.42% |

Year 3, and the environment may change between now and then in terms of level of consumer demand and product interest.").

*Confidence level:*    Relative assessment of the confidence in the data sources and or the information presented (e.g., "The confidence level in this information is high, in that none of it is anecdotal in nature and the revenue stream projections have been validated by an outside source.").

### Approaches

The cost case may incorporate data from outside or inside the organization, but there should be some reference to the validity of the data sources. Some organizations afford a higher level of confidence to information garnered from outside the organization, because it is seen as more objective. The cost case normally will include a financial table of one type or another and should also include a reference to the storage location for that information, as well as who generated it.

Some organizations may omit the interpretive element of the cost case, allowing the numbers to speak for themselves. That can be effective if the organization's culture is relatively static and there is no need to review the existing hurdle rates, thresholds, or corporate sensitivities at some later date.

### Considerations

Cost cases are most common in organizations where strategic issues are not seen as separate and distinct from cost issues. In other words, if a project meets the organization's cost thresholds (in whatever form they take), then the project will move forward. In some organizations, cost information is developed from anecdotal evidence or based on individual relationships between marketing personnel and the customer. Such subjectivity should be documented thoroughly to ensure that any long-term reviews can interpret the original cost case in that context.

## Cost Estimate

### Purpose

The cost estimate is a prediction of project costs either for a phase, the project as a whole, or for the life cycle of the system or product being produced. The cost estimate is most commonly used to determine whether or not the investment in the project will be worthwhile given the perceived gain. It will ultimately contribute to the cost baseline, which is a critical metric for evaluating performance against projections.

### Application

The cost estimate may be developed (and, as such, applied) at a variety of different levels. An initial feasibility estimate (sometimes referred to as a conceptual estimate, "guesstimate," or SWAG) is generally presented as a single number or value representing the overall anticipated cost of the project. It is not broken down into components or subcomponents but normally takes the form of a single monetary figure. Even for this value, there should be some explanation as to the scope of the project, the assumptions made, and the relative time frame for completion, because those considerations will ultimately impact the estimate.

A budget cost estimate (Table 3.2) is perhaps the most common, breaking out the cost estimate into its component parts. This estimate normally includes anticipated resource and material costs, as well as miscellaneous expenses, travel, and organizational overhead.

## Content

The sources for budget information vary widely from organization to organization. Although most hourly/daily rate information and overhead percentages are often available through the accounting or finance departments, the number of hours or materials anticipated for consumption may be drawn out of the resources, out of management projections, or from the imagination of the project manager.

Expense projections can be among the most challenging because they include miscellaneous costs that may be unique to the project and for which historical data may be limited. Travel expenses, for example, can easily be underestimated because they do not normally assume any last-minute travel or supplemental travel requested by the customer.

The estimate confidence level may reflect a best guess by the project manager or may be rooted in extensive statistical analysis based on advanced risk tools such as Monte Carlo analyses. The confidence level affords a relative sense of how sure the project manager is of his numbers and the relative likelihood of hitting the budgetary targets. A low confidence level (e.g., +100%/−100%) indicates a lack of confidence

**Table 3.2**  Budget Cost Estimate

| Cost Type | Utilization Rate | $ per Utilization Rate | Cost Estimate |
|---|---|---|---|
| Resource1 | X hours | $/Hour | X * $ |
| Resource2 | X hours | $/Hour | X * $ |
| Resource3 | X hours | $/Hour | X * $ |
| Resource Subtotal | | | $ |
| Materials1 | X units | $/Unit | X * $ |
| Materials2 | X units | $/Unit | X * $ |
| Materials Subtotal | | $ | |
| Expenses 1 | X units | $/Unit | X * $ |
| Expenses 2 | X units | $/Unit | X * $ |
| Expense Subtotal | | | $ |
| Overhead | | | $ |
|   Resource Overhead | Resource Subtotal * Overhead Percentage | | $ |
|   Material Overhead | Materials Subtotal * Overhead Percentage | | $ |
|   Fringe Benefits | Resource Subtotal * Fringe Percentage | | $ |
| Overhead Subtotal | | | $ |
| Total Project Budget (sum of subtotals) | | | $ |
| Confidence Level | Expressed as a percentage range (e.g., +25/−10%) or as a relative level of confidence (e.g., high, medium, low) | | $ |
| Contingency Budget | Based on confidence level, risk models, organizational project risk practice or other approach | | $ |
| Budget plus Contingency | | | $ |

in the numbers generated through the process. A high confidence level (+10/–5%) indicates a higher degree of certainty in the information provided.

Contingency budgets are used to address those varying levels of confidence and to ensure that the project manager will not be forced to pad other budgetary figures to account for any project unknowns. Invariably, some project issues will surface that require supplemental funding, and if they were part of the original project scope, such issues should be funded through contingency reserves. The level of contingency reserve may be established through confidence level assessments, Monte Carlo analyses, organizational protocols, or risk models.

### Approaches

Cost estimates may follow established organizational formats if they exist. If not, the project manager becomes responsible for ensuring a level of consistency in how the cost estimate information is presented and how the assumptions backing up that cost information are captured. Without effective documentation of that information, the bases for the estimate may be misunderstood (or not considered at all). Consistent formatting and documentation encourages consistent progressive evaluations of the estimates as the project evolves.

### Considerations

Cost estimates are built on the assumption that they will be used as tools for resource and fund allocation by the supporting organization. As such, it is important that they be recognized for what they are—estimates. Estimates cannot divine the future. They provide guidance as to the expectations for project spending. Keeping the estimates realistic can only be accomplished when they are acknowledged as a range of possibilities, rather than a single, absolute figure. There will always be some financial unknowns within any project's budget [3]. The key is to ensure that the budget accounts for both the known and the unknown elements in an open and honest fashion.

## Customer Requirements

### Purpose

The customer requirements delineate, in detail, what the customer needs and how the project will serve those needs. Requirements represent a detailed breakdown of the customer's expectations for the project, as well as how the project organization will serve those requirements. Requirements documentation provides long-term guidance for development of the *work breakdown structure* (WBS) and support for the customer and the project organization as they work toward concurrence on what the project needs to achieve. The customer requirements document serves as an ongoing reference as to what elements of project work are either in scope or out of scope, and in some cases, provides insight into the degree of importance of some elements of scope.

**Application**

Depending on the nature of the document (functional or technical), it will have radically different applications. The functional requirements document addresses the needs of the customer as expressed in terms of performance. The technical requirements document addresses how those needs are to be met. The functional requirements document is outlined in terms of performance, capability, and customer expectations. The technical requirements document is also outlined in those terms, coupled with the technical response about how those needs will be served.

Because of the unique nature of projects, project requirements documents may look different, even when they are generated by the same organization. The template included here is for use as a frame of reference and may lack elements specific to the environment(s) of some organizations, like the NASA version from which it was originally adapted [4].

1.0   Scope
   1.1   System/Product Definition
   1.2   Basic Approach
   1.3   Alternative Approaches
2.0   Documentation Requirements
   2.1   System/Product Documentation
   2.2   Support/Process Documentation
3.0   System/Product Requirements
   3.1   Characteristics/Performance
   3.2   Characteristics/Physical
   3.3   Maintainability/Reliability
4.0   Design, Development, and Construction Requirements
   4.1   Logistics/Maintenance
   4.2   Personnel/Training
5.0   Inspection and Review Requirements
   5.1   Inspections/Validations
   5.2   Reviews/Status
   5.3   Testing
6.0   Packaging/Support
   6.1   Final Preparation
   6.2   Packaging
   6.3   Transition

**Content**

The project requirements document should include details about the specific needs of the project, rather than details about the environment in which they will be developed or the personnel and resources that may be assigned to the project (unless specific resource needs are essential to project success). Again, as was suggested before, the information embedded in this document will vary from project to project, but these are among the core elements that need to be considered. Let's look at the project requirements document outline in a little more detail.

## 1.0   Scope

*1.1   System/Product Definition*   The system/product definition section serves as an overview of what the system or product is to do, including a general description of the use of the system or product by the end user. This information is normally derived from the contract or memorandum of understanding.

*1.2   Basic Approach*   The basic approach section explains how the project organization will develop, produce, organize, or implement the system or product defined in Section 1.1. This information is sometimes described in the project contract or memorandum of understanding, but may also be a product of the project team after the contract has been signed.

*1.3   Alternative Approaches*   The alternative approaches section contains descriptions of alternatives considered or which may be considered if the basic approach (Section 1.2) is deemed unacceptable or unworkable. These are normally developed by the project team as fallback or fail-safe positions, but may also serve simply as evidence that other approaches were considered.

## 2.0   Documentation Requirements

This information on documentation requirements is generated by the project team through interviews, process assessments, contract reviews, and other methods and approved by the project sponsor and/or customer. Documentation is stored centrally to afford access to stakeholders, team members, and functional support on an as-needed basis.

*2.1   System/Product Documentation*   System/product documentation is required to ensure proper implementation or use of the new system, process, or product. The requirements may also include details on the forms and formats the documentation must take.

*2.2   Support/Process Documentation*   Support/process documentation is required during the development of the system, product, or process to provide background, support, status, and development updates. The requirements should delineate not only the type of documentation, but the frequency with which it should be generated. This will also include the process for approvals and acceptance of documentation, status communications, and change order documentation.

## 3.0   System/Product Requirements

System/product information is generated by the project team through interviews, evaluations, feasibility studies, and other methods and approved by the project sponsor and/or customer. Documentation is stored centrally to afford access to stakeholders, team members, and functional support on an as-needed basis.

*3.1   Characteristics/Performance*   The characteristics/performance section deals with how the system, product, or process should perform and to what degree. This may come from the original contract or memorandum of understanding, but must be documented sufficiently to clarify what is/is not acceptable performance for the project deliverable(s).

*3.2 Characteristics/Physical* Details on what the system, product, or process should look, feel, taste, sound, and smell like are provided in the characteristics/physical section. This may come from the original contract or memorandum of understanding but must be documented sufficiently to clarify what are/are not acceptable physical attributes for the project deliverable(s).

*3.3 Maintainability/Reliability* The maintainability/reliability details describe the level of effort required to keep the project deliverable(s) functional to a level acceptable to the customer and/or end user. This should include any specific long-term maintenance expectations as well as a perspective on the life span of the deliverable(s).

## 4.0 Design, Development, and Construction Requirements

*4.1 Logistics/Maintenance* Facilities, material, and organizational support required during the design and development phases are covered by the logistics/maintenance section. This may include specifications as to what property will be furnished by the client organization and what logistics will be managed by the project organization.

*4.2 Personnel/Training* Training and personnel support required during the design and development phases are documented here. This includes personnel needs from both the client and project organizations and any training required to facilitate their efforts during project design and development.

## 5.0 Inspection and Review Requirements

*5.1 Inspections/Validations* The inspections/validations section documents any mandated inspections or validations that were established contractually.

*5.2 Reviews/Status* The review/status section includes any regular reviews, status reports, progress reports, forecasts, or other project assessments required by both the client and project organizations. The requirements should delineate not only the type of documentation, but the frequency with which it should be generated and to whom it goes. (In some instances, this will overlap with or replace Section 2.2.)

*5.3 Testing* Any system, process, or deliverables testing established contractually or required by virtue of organizational protocol is documented here. This should include details on the frequency of any such tests.

## 6.0 Packaging/Support

*6.1 Final Preparation* The final preparation section details any steps required to take the finished deliverables from their production state to implementation. This may include expectations in terms of packing, crating, formatting, or final presentation.

*6.2 Packaging* In some instances, this section will be a reiteration of Section 6.1. In others it will determine the long-term packaging requirements for the deliverables as they are transmitted to the customer and/or end user.

*6.3 Transition* The transition section includes any lingering training, conversion, or delivery issues. It also defines the maintainability criteria (a metric or performance level required once the system is in operation) and any specific means for quality control after the project is handed off and in operation. This also often includes a list of the final signatories on a project and/or deliverable acceptance.

### Approaches

Some organizations use the project requirements documentation as a catch-all tool for every issue from project risk to change control. Because the term *requirements* reaches across the breadth of the project, such applications are not unreasonable. Although the requirements document *may* capture a wide range of issues, however, it should focus on the needs that much be met to ensure project success.

### Considerations

In building the project requirements document, managers may be tempted to fill in every field, even when the information is not yet available. If information is lacking for a particular component of the template, it is prudent to document such information as "currently unavailable," rather than filling the void with guess-work. If guesses are mixed with the validated project information, it becomes challenging to discern which information is real and current and which is the author's best guess.

## Feasibility Analysis

### Purpose

The feasibility analysis is designed to determine whether or not, given the project environment, a project will be successful (in virtually *any* interpretation of that word). A feasibility analysis may be conducted for a project with an emphasis on financial viability, environmental integrity, cultural acceptability, or political practicability. It is a determination as to the likelihood of success and a description of how that determination was achieved.

### Application

Feasibility analyses are used to present an approach or a series of alternatives and to offer decision-making guidance based on the climate in which the project will evolve. They often defend a single or primary approach, incorporating extensive forecasts on the project's development, as well as its evolution after implementation. Because a feasibility analysis may focus on one or many aspects of a project, it may be a very short (one- to two-page) or long (multivolume) document. In any case, it generally begins with an executive summary and a description of the project outputs in their as-built condition.

A basic preproject feasibility analysis might include the following:

1.0   Executive Summary/Project Goal
2.0   Project Description
   2.1   Anticipated As-Built Condition
   2.2   Anticipated Outputs
3.0   Project Environment

3.1   Financial
3.2   Physical Environment
3.3   Societal/Cultural Environment
4.0   Similar Efforts
    4.1   Scenarios
    4.2   Similarities and Implications
5.0   Sensitivity Analyses
    5.1   Financial
    5.2   Physical Environment
    5.3   Social/Cultural Environment
6.0   Marketing/Public Relations
    6.1   Market Analysis
    6.2   Forecasts
    6.3   Competitive Environment
    6.4   Risk
7.0   Conclusions and Recommendations

**Content**

The sources for content in a feasibility analysis come through extensive research, discussion, and assessment and may incorporate the use of advanced computer modeling to determine the long-term impact of a project on the environment around it. Other feasibility analyses may be rooted only in anecdotal evidence as provided by those who have worked on similar efforts or those who will ultimately be affected by the project's outcome.

### 1.0   Executive Summary/Project Goal

Overview or description of the impact of the project on its environment and the potential for success (or failure) based on the analysis. This may also include brief mention of the alternatives considered and their relative viability.

### 2.0   Project Description

*2.1   Anticipated As-Built Condition*   This section is a description of the project as envisioned, including magnitude, location, community impact, and market change.

*2.2   Anticipated Outputs*   In this section, both intended and consequential outputs of the project should be incorporated, without comment as to their relative benefit or detriment to the world around them.

### 3.0   Project Environment

*3.1   Financial*   This section describes the financial climate in which the project will be developed and in which it will be implemented. This may include assessments of the relative magnitude of the project within the overall organizational budget and the potential drain on available resources.

*3.2  Physical Environment*    A feasibility analysis should include a description of the environment surrounding the project, including the physical locations for development and implementation.

*3.3  Societal/Cultural Environment*    Descriptions of the culture and society in and around the project community are another aspect to a feasibility analysis. This may include an emphasis on those social and cultural issues that will be directly affected by project development and implementation.

## 4.0   Similar Efforts

*4.1  Scenarios*    The section provides an outline of similar efforts and a synopsis of their effects on the finances and physical and social environments of their project organizations and communities.

*4.2  Similarities and Implications*    Determination of the degree of similarity between the scenarios outlined in Section 4.1 and the project(s) under scrutiny in the feasibility analysis is discussed in this section. All significant discrepancies among examples should be noted.

## 5.0   Sensitivity Analyses

*5.1  Financial*    A "what-if" analysis of finances to determine if the project is deemed viable is an important aspect of a feasibility analysis. An assessment of other organizational areas affected is included. This analysis may also examine the potential range of financial possibilities if the project fares extremely well or poorly.

*5.2  Physical Environment*    This section involves a "what-if" analysis of the physical environment if the project is deemed viable. It includes an assessment of physical effects to the organization and the areas around the project. This analysis may also examine the potential range of physical manifestations if the project fares extremely well or poorly.

*5.3  Social/Cultural Environment*    The section is a "what-if" analysis of the social and cultural environment if the project is deemed viable. It includes an assessment of the effects to local, regional, national, and international societies. This analysis may also address the potential range of social and cultural implications if the project fares extremely well or poorly.

## 6.0   Marketing/Public Relations

*6.1  Market Analysis*    The market analysis includes an assessment of the potential market for the project or its outputs, including (but not limited to) the financial buying power of the market, interest in or demand for the project, and the life span of the market's potential members.

*6.2  Forecasts*    Predictions regarding sales, returns, and buying trends related to the project and its outputs are included in the forecasting section. Ideally, the forecast includes the timing of the market entry and the relative impact of early or late entry into the marketplace.

*6.3  Competitive Environment*    The competitive environment section contains information on other organizations capable of conducting the project and/or producing its deliverables (or their equivalent). This may also incorporate some assessment of how potentially fickle the market may be about the project or its deliverables.

*6.4  Risk*    Major risks should be considered in any feasibility analysis. They include those that could radically alter any or all of the assumptions on which the feasibility assessment is based and the potential market impact if those risks come to pass.

### 7.0  Conclusions and Recommendations

Based on the information from the analysis, this section discusses the conclusions that can be drawn regarding the viability (or nonviability) of the project, given the environment in which it will be developed and implemented. This normally includes a go/no-go decision and the implications of both of those decisions.

### Approaches

Some feasibility analyses will include extensive discussions on the project plan for how and when the project will evolve and the expectations during development. Some will go into extensive detail about the side effects of the project both during development and implementation. Because feasibility analyses are developed for everything from new business methodologies to power plant installations, the range of possibilities in terms of what they may include is virtually endless. The key to determining if information is appropriate in a feasibility analysis is to assess whether or not the information provided helps to generate a more accurate understanding of whether or not the project will succeed in implementation, regardless of the metric for success.

### Considerations

Because projects are undertaken with sponsors and supporters, the feasibility analysis will promote a particular point of view or perspective in making the go/no-go decision. It is to the author's advantage to minimize the politicization of the feasibility analysis, because *any* skewing of the data may be seen as rendering the rest of the document and its findings moot.

## Forecasts

### Purpose

Forecasts are used to assess potential future business performance. They are predictions as to the outcomes of a project. They provide project managers and their management insight on how well the project is expected to perform in terms of cost, schedule, or overall deliverable performance. They also identify the range of possible outcomes for planning purposes.

### Application

Because of their varied applications, forecasts may take on a variety of forms. They may provide a graphic perspective on the likelihood of completion within a given time frame (as depicted in Figure 3.1). They may also include information from a

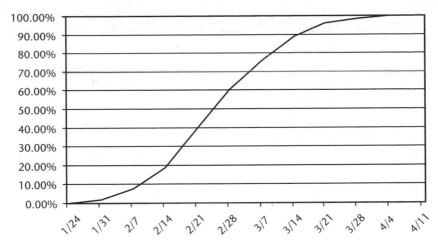

**Figure 3.1**    Schedule forecast.

statistical sampling or Monte Carlo analysis, providing information on the number of samples that met a certain time or cost projection (as shown in Figure 3.2), or they may simply be statements of intended or expected outcomes, highlighting the elements that may have the greatest direct impact on the accuracy of the forecast (Table 3.3).

## Content

The content sources for forecasts are dependent on the type of forecast in question. For statistical analyses and projections, Monte Carlo analyses and other forecasting tools may be used. Tools like Computer Associates' *Risk-Plus* or Palisades' *@Risk* develop the curves based on the available project and statistical information on a task-by-task or work package-by-work package basis. Monte Carlo tools process the individual task information and create a series of samples to determine the relative likelihood of particular outcomes. Although only one outcome is ultimately

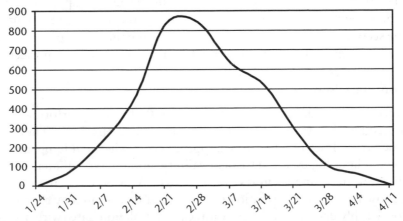

**Figure 3.2**    Cost forecast.

**Table 3.3**　Sample of a Simple Forecast of Intended Outcomes

| Project Title | |
|---|---|
| | Source/Rationale: |
| Original Completion Date: | Project Plan |
| Projected Completion Date: | |
| Original Project Budget: | Project Plan |
| Projected Project Expenditures: | |
| Original Milestone 1 Date: | Project Plan |
| Projected Milestone 1 Date: | |
| Original Milestone 2 Date: | |
| Projected Performance Variance: | |

possible, Monte Carlo generates hundreds or thousands of samples to provide a curve illustrating the time or cost targets with the highest probability of occurrence.

For less statistically driven analyses, projections are often provided by individuals performing the work or by those familiar with the nature of the work and who have assessed progress to date. In addition to time and cost projections, these analyses may also incorporate some assessment of project performance and deliverable performance, particularly because it may vary from the original assessments and projections. This information is frequently provided by individuals who understand the nature of the work and the progress to date. Anyone providing performance information should be intimately familiar with customer expectations, the contract (or statement of work or memorandum of understanding), the business case, and the nature of the work completed to date. The performance aspects of a forecast are largely speculative, unless product or project performance is directly tied to measurable criteria, which are linked directly to intermediate deliverables.

## Approaches

Forecasts may be narrative and/or graphic in nature and may take a short- or long-term perspective. Because they are predictive by nature, the level of perceived accuracy should be noted to differentiate between wild guesses and information rooted in statistical depth. If the forecasts are provided as a component of a larger reporting requirement, they may include a schedule for the next reassessment. If the forecast is the second or later in a series, it may be accompanied by a previous forecast, coupled with an explanation for any dramatic shifts from previous projections.

## Considerations

A forecast is a glance into the "crystal ball" of project performance. Some forecasts are couched in such a way that they sound like absolutes. They are not. They are studied analyses of what *may* happen, versus what *will* happen. The data sources, the methodologies, the statistical validity, and the type of analysis will all influence the look, feel, and accuracy of a forecast. As a practical matter, some forecasters choose to present information precisely as it is generated by the tools. Because many tools apply detailed statistics, a forecast completion date (with a specific percentage level of certainty) may be generated down to the day, hour, minute, and second. Budget forecasts from such tools often are presented to the penny. Although such apparent accuracy is impressive, it does not convey the nature of a forecast as a prediction. It creates an impression of certainty where no certainty exists. Such false precision should be considered carefully before the information is incorporated into a forecast.

## Impact Analysis

### Purpose

An impact analysis looks at the outcome(s) of a project and its (their) potential effect on the environment around the project (business environment, physical environment, financial environment, political environment, and so on). At the very least, an impact analysis will highlight the differences in the environment between the status quo and the environment after the project has been implemented. At the extreme, the impact analysis may look at a host of gradients of project impact, as well as the impacts of alternative approaches.

### Application

An impact analysis can be used to either heighten or allay concerns about a project's outcome by focusing on postproject conditions. It can be applied either prior to or after the project has been implemented. If developed prior to the project, any assumptions used to determine postproject conditions should be clearly stipulated and any tools applied to ascertain the future state should be identified. If developed *after* the project has been implemented, the sources for any historical information regarding the preproject state should be acknowledged as well.

An impact analysis incorporates the following components:

- Anticipated outcomes from project;
- Preproject state;
- Areas where the project is/was expected to impact the preproject state;
- Assumptions;
- Data sources;
- Data presentation (preproject versus postproject);
- Conclusions.

### Content

The content for an impact analysis is most commonly quantitative in nature. Qualitative impact analyses are not unheard of, but they often have the air of a simple defense of a single point of view. In some instances, qualitative assessments will be converted to quantitative values through preordained metrics or surveys. In any case, the effort should be to keep the assessments as objective as possible.

As for the components of the analysis, the content comes from a variety of sources:

- *Anticipated outcomes from project.* This information may come from the project plan, the customer statement of work, requirements documentation, or feasibility studies done on the project. This is normally an objective statement (in a few paragraphs) that serves as an overview of project intent.
- *Preproject state.* This is an assessment (historical or present day) of the critical environment(s) as it(they) existed prior to project implementation. Any existing statistical data on performance or condition should be presented here.
- *Areas where the project is/was expected to impact the preproject state.* This identifies the environment(s) where an impact is expected to occur, in terms of changes in process, approach, outcome, or perception.
- *Assumptions.* Perhaps the single most critical element, the assumptions frequently determine the validity (or invalidity) of the impact analysis. Any assumptions regarding the preproject state, impact, postproject state, or the data should be defined in detail. Any efforts that were made to validate the assumptions should also be documented.
- *Data sources.* The data sources should be defined, as well as the time when the data were gathered and the methodology for gathering them. Any assumptions used to fill data gaps or to gather the data should be reflected under in the assumptions section (see previous entry).
- *Data presentation (preproject versus postproject).* Often in tabular format, data regarding the preproject and postproject states should be juxtaposed for easy review.
- *Conclusions.* Although the data should be presented in such a fashion that the conclusions are self-evident, any specific conclusions the reader is expected to draw should be affirmed at the end of the analysis. If some of the conclusions draw on assumptions, those assumptions should have been identified earlier in the document and should be reasserted here.

### Approaches

Impact analysis can focus on a single issue or on multiple issues, although a multiple-issue impact analysis can become unwieldy. The challenge in dealing with multiple effects to a single environment (or more confusing, multiple environments) is that the data can become a sea of numbers with very little cogent insight to be drawn from them. If the data are largely qualitative, the methodology for its development will be crucial. The more insight that can be developed about where the numbers came from, the better.

### Considerations

In conducting a review of an impact analysis, the first questions always relate to the data—too much? Too little? That is a major issue. Too much data will leave the reviewer believing that there is information hidden that she does not understand. Too little data will look like the impact analysis was incomplete. There should be sufficient data to support a single story or premise, without bludgeoning the reader with it.

Also, in establishing the assumptions, the author of the impact analysis should determine how the assumptions might be misconstrued or misunderstood. What if the reader does not agree with the assumptions? If those questions can be defined and clarified, their answers should be provided as a component of the impact analysis.

## Mission Statement

### Purpose

At the project or organizational level, a mission statement provides a single-sentence (or single-paragraph) encapsulation of the objective. The mission statement serves as a guidepost for action, establishing where the organization (or project) is supposed to be going.

### Application

The mission statement is normally used as a public pronouncement, posted prominently to declare organizational intent. It is not used for detailed planning, but instead as a validation of any approaches, processes, or deliverables in terms of strategic direction. The forms for such statements are relatively consistent.

[Organization][provides, conducts, constructs, develops, creates, enhances] [services, products, deliverables] for [purpose or recipient] to [rationale]. [Benefits]

### Content

The content for an organizational mission statement is normally developed at the senior levels of the organization, expressing their intent for the long-term goals. The content for a project mission statement is normally developed by the project manager and his team, expressing their desired project goal and how its deliverables will serve the intended body of stakeholders.

The mission statement for the United States National Weather Service states:

The National Weather Service (NWS) provides weather, hydrologic, and climate forecasts and warnings for the United States, its territories, adjacent waters and ocean areas, for the protection of life and property and the enhancement of the national economy. NWS data and products form a national information database and infrastructure which can be used by other governmental agencies, the private sector, the public, and the global community.

This example provides a sense of the mission statement's ability to capture the deliverables and processes to be followed, as well as the potential boundaries of what is (and what is not) within the organization's scope.

### Approaches

The mission statement can be developed either from a strategic perspective or by examining current organizational practice. From a strategic perspective, the responsible parties (senior management at the organizational level; project management at the project level) identify what they hope to accomplish or achieve. Rather than focusing on detailed deliverables, they look at the general outcomes and the practices required to get there.

From a practical perspective, if there is no guiding strategy, the mission statement can be developed by looking at what the organization produces and identifying the commonalities therein. Ideally, those commonalities should reflect the organization's intent, as well as acceptable and/or desirable practice to achieve that intent.

### Considerations

In some organizations, the mission statement is touted by management as a guiding force and is used in virtually all aspects of decision making. Staff members of the U.S. Defense Finance and Accounting Service (DFAS), for example, actually carry around their organization's mission statement on small blue cards at virtually all times. In organizations where that level of zeal in using the mission statement is apparent, consistency will be crucial. By contrast, in organizations where the mission statement is largely a management exercise with little organizational impact, a higher level of flexibility may be deemed acceptable. The longer a mission statement is in place, communicated, and promoted, the greater its potential impact.

## Organization Chart

### Purpose

As with the mission statement, the organization chart may be developed at the project or organizational level. At the organizational level, the chart is used to define the hierarchy of who works for whom and to delineate the reporting structure of the organization. At the project level, the organization chart may focus slightly more on who works *with* whom, in terms of project task integration.

### Application

Organization charts are used to communicate the staff hierarchy. They are publicly available and provide staff with the ability to see the chain of command from the worker level up to the highest levels of management. Some organization charts may be used to determine peer status with other components of the organization.

### Content

The traditional organization chart (as depicted in Figure 3.3) identifies the chain of command, as well as the peer-to-peer hierarchy. By virtue of the depth of the reporting levels, the vice presidents in Figure 3.3 know that they are all at the same relative level of importance; the same is true of the managers beneath them.

A project organization chart is virtually identical in structure, but it may differ if it is broken down by deliverables, as well as function (because the two are often congruent in nature) (see Figure 3.4).

Some project managers may link the organization chart directly to the WBS, creating an organizational breakdown structure of the work to be performed. However, the depth of information provided in an organization chart is limited.

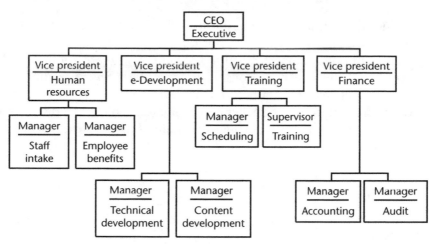

**Figure 3.3** Sample organization chart.

## Approaches

The way in which the organization chart is broken down is largely a matter of personal preference, although professional need may enter into the decision. Because the project organization chart can be broken down by function *or* deliverable, the question should be asked as to which approach provides the greater understanding of the project and the interactions of those serving the project. Some organization charts may feature dotted or broken lines representing secondary reporting relationships. A clear legend should accompany the organization chart if alternative types of relationships are displayed in the chart.

## Considerations

While the organization chart is a simple graphic depiction, it carries a great deal of political weight. In the project organization chart, personnel may find themselves

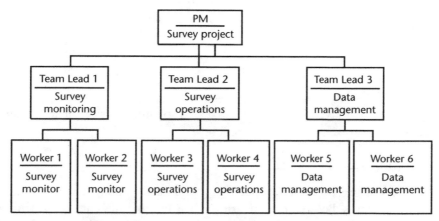

**Figure 3.4** Project organization chart.

outside their traditional organizational hierarchy and directly aligned with individuals with whom they do not normally work. That sometimes causes some measure of political angst, because individuals who are not normally perceived as peers may have a peer relationship in the project. In the traditional organization chart, any movement of a box, line or level can have significant ramifications on how staff members perceive themselves and their roles. As a rule, it is advantageous to limit the number of reporting lines going "up" the chart from any individual staff member.

## Press Kits

### Purpose

Press kits are a key component of a press briefing, normally held to inform members of the media about a new project or the status of the project, its environment, or its supporting organization. They are intended to present the project organization (or host organization) in the best possible light.

### Application

Press kits are constructed when a project or its impact is sufficiently signifi-cant that public information campaigns using mass media are appropriate. They should be developed whenever the project has achieved sufficient recognition that the project organization's perspective on the effort will be deemed to be of public interest or when the press requests information on the project. Keep in mind that public recognition may be positive or negative in nature, and may be proactive or reactive, depending on the nature of the project and the project organization.

### Content

Content for a press kit should be determined well in advance of any press briefing to ensure that the correct information is shared and any information that the organi-zation does *not* want to share is clearly defined for those hosting the briefing. The press kits will highlight corporate history, general information, past press releases, and any contact persons' business cards. They may also include small product samples, as appropriate. The press kit should include a press release (see the following).

### Approach

A press kit may be an in-depth package of information or a few sheets of paper detailing future plans and approaches.

### Considerations

Press kits are normally prepackaged and easily updated with the latest corporate press releases. Because organizational history does not change overnight, most of the information in a press kit can be retained for long periods of time.

# Press Release

## Purpose

A press release is issued to provide public awareness on an issue of importance to the organization. It serves as a formal expression of the organization's stance on that issue, and frequently provides commentary from someone in the upper echelons of the organizational hierarchy. It may be in response to environmental conditions affecting the organization or may be initiated to promote the organization's perspective.

## Application

Press releases are used to encourage favorable media coverage of the organization. They are used by the media, either in whole or part, as a component of news or public service coverage. They may be used as written, but are frequently rewritten to fit the style of the media outlet. Because major media outlets may receive hundreds of press releases in a given day, releases are often managed by large media services, who channel the information to as many outlets as possible. Some press releases are accompanied by media information kits, providing background information, samples, or novelties to encourage more in-depth or favorable coverage.

## Content

A press release normally includes a headline, contact information, a dateline, and the body of a story that the organization considers of interest to the public (or to the intended audience). It is normally written using newspaper-style guidelines to facilitate its use without significant editing. The top third of the page should contain most of the information essential for an editor to make a decision as to whether or not the story is appropriate for use. The content should reflect the traditional depth of understanding of the intended audience. For instance, the content of a press release for a local newspaper may be less in depth than the treatment of the same story for a professional journal or trade magazine.

> Contact Name: *Jane Doe, Public Relations Officer, Alpha Corporation*
> Contact Phone: *+1 (301) 555-1212*
> Contact E-mail: *jdoe@alpha.com*
> Contact Mail: *Jane Doe*
> *Alpha Corporation Public Relations*
> *315 Parkview Drive*
> *Alpha, MD 44445*
>
> *ALPHA ANNOUNCES SEWAGE TREATMENT BREAKTHROUGH*
>
> *May 29, 2007 (Alpha, Maryland) "It's a new day in sewage." Alpha Corporation President John Roe says the company's new treatment technologies will eliminate...*

## Approaches

The tone or tenor of the news item should reflect its general level of acceptance in the public. Because most press releases are written to generate favorable press attention (rather than to deflect negative attention), the releases will start on a positive tone, highlighting the most significant achievement or accomplishment the release is designed to tout. In the case where a press release is issued defensively (in response to media attacks or negative public attention), the tone of the release should be more conciliatory, first acknowledging the concern, and then refuting, defending, or accepting the organization's role.

Given the sheer volume of press releases received by some media outlets, some organizations choose to present their information innovatively, using CDs, pop-ups (paper and virtual), and other gimmicks to gain attention. One Maryland brick manufacturer actually mailed customized bricks to media outlets in an effort to gain attention for their company's fiftieth anniversary.

### Considerations

Different media outlets have different needs. Newspapers need attractive, high-quality graphics. Some newspapers prefer color, while others continue to work exclusively in black and white. Radio stations prefer colorful spokespersons who can be engaging in sound bites of less than 30 seconds. Talk-oriented radio stations may also prefer spokespersons who can talk for 30 minutes or more, as the format allows. Television stations prefer the short sound bites, but also lean toward those individuals who can make themselves available either on site or in studio. Magazines tend to prefer very high quality graphics coupled with a longer release format.

Press releases rarely stand on their own. There is normally some degree of follow-up by media outlets before the story is used. The accessibility to the media of the contact person will be crucial to successful application.

## Project Charter

### Purpose

The project charter is a foundation communications tool in project management. It serves to grant the project manager the authority that she needs to manage resources and to clarify the scope of the project (in general terms). In theory, it is drafted by senior management as their means to clarify roles and responsibilities among their staff, but in practice it is most frequently developed by the project manager, who then directs it to management for their approval.

### Application

The charter is used as a reference document to affirm the level of resource commitment and organizational support for a project. After it is created, it is maintained by the project manager, and provided to functional managers on request to confirm intended resource utilization and rationale.

### Content

The charter normally incorporates a general scope statement, as well as a list of the resources that will be applied to support the project objective. It may include both internal and external resources, as well as the signature(s) authorizing their use through the life of the project. The charter should also include a specific time frame in which those resources will be applied, indicating when they will be returned to their traditional or functional responsibilities.

### Approaches

Charters are constructed to varying levels of depth, based on the needs of the organization. Table 3.4 shows one approach to creating a sample project charter.

### Considerations

Because the project charter is designed to provide the project manager with the authority necessary to carry out the project, it should be viewed as a politically sensitive document. Some functional managers will balk at requirements that they sign the charter because they may view it as "signing away" their authority over resources. The charter objective should be written to such a level of detail that it becomes clear the resources will only be "on loan" to the project, rather than committed to it for the remainder of their tenure with the organization. If the charter is not accompanied by signatures, it may not have the political weight necessary for the project manager to successfully execute the project.

**Table 3.4**    Sample Project Charter

| | |
|---|---|
| *Project Name* | |
| *Project objective/scope statement* | The project objective should include the specific goals or deliverables the project is expected to produce; it may incorporate the deadline and anticipated budget at completion. It should be stated as unambiguously as possible and may cross-reference any specific sources for additional information or detail. |
| *Notes on the objective* | There may be supplemental information appropriate to the objective, specifically including, but not limited to, a list of any activities that are specifically not covered by the objective (e.g., "the project shall not include predevelopment analysis of . . ."). |
| *Resources to be applied to the project* | Human resources (internal)—Any functional staff temporarily assigned to the project<br>Human resources (external)—Any temporary hires or consulting staff assigned to the project<br>Material resources (temporary)—Any material resources on loan for the duration of the project, including special facilities<br>Material resources (permanent)—Any material resources committed to the project, intended to remain with the new project owner |
| *Delegation of authority* | A clear statement regarding the level of authority granted to the project manager for the duration of the project, indicating his or her ability to coordinate, schedule, and support resources during the project's implementation. |
| *Release date* | Anticipated completion date of the project and/or release date for internal and temporary resources. |
| *Signatures* | Signatures of senior management authorizing the project and (in some instances) functional managers releasing resources for project use. |

## Project Proposal

### Purpose

The project proposal is a preproject document that recommends a project for initiation, provides a rationale for the project, and suggests approaches and staffing. The proposal is an early component of project documentation that serves to launch the project. It does not necessarily consider or incorporate the entire technical solution for the project, but does offer a suggestion that the project is appropriate, necessary, and worthwhile.

### Application

Less detailed than a formal feasibility study or analysis, the project proposal is intended to raise awareness that a project may be appropriate and viable. It can be used at almost any level of the organization and is usually drafted by a team member or senior executive. At a minimum, it provides a general description of what the project is supposed to accomplish and how or when it could be implemented. At the extreme, it may describe not only the project deliverables, but the approach, the resources to be applied, and the alternative approaches that could be used for implementation. It is used to present ideas to anyone responsible for project selection and to initiate the selection process.

### Content

The project proposal defends a particular perspective or approach to solving a problem or creating a solution. Some of the items, as noted in the following list, may be considered "optional" content for the project proposal. However, they will ultimately have to be included in some project analysis before a final go/no-go determination is made. The project proposal should incorporate the following items:

- Name of the project;
- Initiator;
- Project sponsor/champion (optional);
- Technical/support organization (optional);
- Project description and justification;
- Recommended manager/resources;
- Project budget/schedule (optional).

### Approaches

The information embedded in the project proposal is often couched as a sales pitch or enticement to encourage other members of the organization to support the effort. Even so, the information included in the proposal should be presented as objectively as possible to allow for independent assessment of the validity of the suggestion(s) included therein.

- *Name of the project.* This should be descriptive, rather than creative. Instead of the "Gruntilator 1400," the name might be "Exercise Equipment Station."

- *Initiator*. This is the author of the project proposal, including name, function, and contact information.
- *Project sponsor/champion (optional)*. Provide the name of the senior management or executive level authority supporting the project's initiation.
- *Technical/support organization (optional)*. As appropriate, list the name of the functional organization primarily responsible for project implementation.
- *Project description and justification*. Provide a general description of the project, including the impetus for implementation.
- *Recommended manager/resources*. List any specific resources or resource skill sets required for project success, as well as the rationale for their selection.
- *Project budget/schedule (optional)*. As appropriate and available, this information, if included, should be provided with a relative range of accuracy to denote the confidence level in the numbers provided.

### Considerations

The project proposal is most commonly an internal document. But because it proposes a change to current business or operating practices, it may be considered a politically volatile document. In developing the project proposal, the more and higher the levels of sponsorship and support, the more likely it is to be received favorably.

## Project Request

### Purpose

Because different organizations interpret project requests (as a practice) differently, their purposes may vary as well. A project request may be a simple one-paragraph description of a project that has been formally submitted to management (either through a chartering process or proposal process). It may also be a specific form or format for submitting initial information about a project that may be of interest to the organization or that may serve an organizational need. For the sake of this discussion, the latter is assumed.

### Application

A project request is used as a means to initiate ongoing analysis (feasibility study, impact analysis) of a project concept. Information available for the project request is generally somewhat scant, as the project request is used only to trigger other processes.

### Content

A project request form includes only the most rudimentary information about a project concept:

- Project name (or a few-word description);

- Project description (may include a brief description of the goals or objectives of the project, as well as any problems/concerns it is designed to resolve);
- Timing;
- Special resource needs (may include material or human resources essential to project initiation or implementation);
- Support organization (the anticipated "home" for the project if it is determined to be viable);
- Name of person completing the form.

Although other information may be incorporated, these are the essentials for initiating a project and ensure that a consistent baseline set of information is available for any project that will undergo further study or scrutiny.

### Approaches

The information embedded here may be redundant with information collected for a project proposal or feasibility analysis. That is why, particularly in smaller organizations, a project request form may be embedded within those other processes. Larger organizations use project request forms as an initial screening mechanism to enter projects into the process and to ensure that those that undergo more formal feasibility assessment are initiated at the appropriate levels within the organization.

### Considerations

Because the project request form data are frequently redundant with information gathered in other processes, it should be applied only when there are copious requests being filed on a regular basis, the organization is large, and tracking mechanisms are limited. In smaller organizations where project owners are easily identified, project requests may be seen as purely administrative overhead.

## Quality Policy

### Purpose

With the advent of the national and international passion for quality (as evidenced by such efforts as the Malcolm Baldrige award) [5], project managers have been under pressure to ensure that their projects serve the same quality standards demanded by their organizations for more conventional efforts. As such, quality policy statements have come into vogue, delineating what is important to the organization from a quality perspective and the degree(s) to which the project will serve those objectives.

### Application

The quality policy is used to express the intangible nature of quality to the team, the customer, and management in such a way that those parties can understand the extent to which the organization will go in meeting project goals and objectives. It is normally used to establish boundaries as to what is or is not acceptable and may also provide guidance on how unacceptable projects or components may be brought into alignment with the policy. In some instances, it will be used to emphasize *how* the work will be accomplished as well as the nature of the deliverables themselves.

## Content

A quality policy incorporates the elements discussed in the following subsections.

### 1.0   Purpose/Rationale/Background

In an effort to establish the rationale for a given quality perspective, the quality policy normally includes a background statement, defining how or why a certain degree of quality was deemed appropriate.

### 2.0   Quality Policy Statement

This may be a one-line general policy statement or a detailed analysis of what constitutes quality on projects in general or on a given project in particular. As an example, the Goddard Space Flight Center quality policy has both. Their one-line statement, "GSFC is committed to meeting or exceeding our customers' requirements" [6], provides very limited, general guidance, while their multivolume quality management system provides depth on what "meeting or exceeding" means.

In the ideal, the quality policy statement will provide some insight that specifically directs the types of behaviors involved.

### 3.0   Support

This should be a statement as to who serves as the arbiter of "quality" under the policy and who is the author or owner of the policy.

## Approaches

In the ideal project environment, the quality policy will incorporate both a general statement about anticipated level of quality, as well as how that level of quality will be achieved. The U.S. Army's Department of Laboratory Sciences (serving in the European theater) has a quality policy that both references specific compliance standards they follow as well as guidance on *how* to follow them.

> We want to create an environment and provide resources that encourage the highest ethical and professional practices suited to the following objectives:
>
> - Produce quality analytical data by
>   - maintaining competent well-trained staff through external and internal training opportunities,
>   - monitoring laboratory performance through data review and validation, equipment maintenance and verification, and the QC and PT programs, and
>   - the continuous review of the QMS to identify areas for improvement with QSR and MRT meetings, internal and external audits, and corrective and preventive actions.
> - Provide excellent service to our customers by
>   - partnering with our contractors and vendors to provide the best supplies and laboratory information available,

- carefully planning our work and services to meet specified requirements, Data Quality Objectives (DQOs), and/or Memorandum of Understanding (MOU) for projects, products, or contracts,

- seeking feedback from our customers on how we can improve our service to them through customer surveys, meetings, or telephone consults, and providing feedback and follow-up to them, and

- assisting each other to go above and beyond in all aspects of our work in order to delight the customer.

All DLS personnel are required to be thoroughly familiar with the necessary QMS documentation and fully implement the quality policies and procedures in every aspect of their work. This policy shall be reviewed by the MRT on an annual basis, or as required for continuing suitability. The Quality Policy statement is issued under the authority of the DLS laboratory and technical director (chief executive). [7]

The DLS quality policy statement is noteworthy for the level of depth and approaches that it specifies may be used and for establishing some of the basic procedures that may support the policy.

### Considerations

Quality policies and policy statements may be implemented at the project or organizational level. It may not be necessary for the project manager to generate or create a separate quality policy statement for each project. However, if the project is venturing into new territory for the organization, some direction on the level of quality or general performance may be appropriate. In instances where a clear organizational quality policy already exists, it is perfectly sufficient and reasonable to simply reiterate it in the context of the project to reinforce it with the project team.

## Risk Models

### Purpose

Risk models are designed to provide a consistent up-front assessment of the relative levels of risk and opportunity associated with a given project. They are also used to highlight any specific risk areas endemic within the organization. The models provide an at-a-glance risk assessment without the detailed qualitative and quantitative analyses typical of later stages in the project.

### Application

Risk models consist of a series of questions or objective assessments related to the risk posture of the organization. The questions may be simple binary assessments (e.g., "Have the project requirements been developed and traced into the WBS?") or weighted evaluations (e.g., "What percentage of the requirements have been developed and traced into the WBS?"). In either case, the organization-critical risks are presented in a consistent format so the answers from one project may be compared with the answers from another. This relative evaluation can serve a variety of functions. It can be used to identify areas of risk specific to the project. It can provide a sense of the relative need for management attention from one project to the other. It can be used to establish contingency budgets, because those projects with higher risk may merit higher cost or schedule contingencies.

## Content

Some risk models may simply include a massive list of questions, where the greater number of "high-risk" responses indicates a higher level of overall project risk. One of the most exhaustive such lists was generated by the Software Engineering Institute in their *Taxonomy-Based Risk Identification* [8] incorporating almost 200 questions relevant to the potential risks associated with any project.

Other models will include more organizationally specific content, focusing on the nature of risks (and sometimes opportunities) within the organization. In those types of models, the risks are often weighted according to their relative levels of importance as in the following example:

> *Risk Area:* REGULATORY COMPLIANCE (Weight: 8)
> *High (3)*—Project is subject to multijurisdictional reviews/regulations.
> *Medium (2)*—Project is subject to regulations from a single jurisdiction.
> *Low (1)*—No regulatory influence.
> *Risk Area:* DATA SECURITY (Weight: 4)
> *High (3)*—Data will be made available via the Internet.
> *Medium (2)*—Data will be made available via networked terminals.
> *Low (1)*—Data will be available only within the "closed" system.

Projects are assessed by reviewing their condition and multiplying that score by the weight of the issue under consideration. A project facing multijurisdictional reviews, for example, would merit a risk score of 24 on that issue. A project facing multijurisdictional reviews *and* presenting information over the Internet would have a total score of 36 (Regulatory Compliance Score: 24 + Data Security Score: 12).

The content is determined by management teams as being the areas that pose the greatest potential threat to the organization or to the project in terms of long-term success. The objective assessment criteria should be established by teams who know and understand the nature of the organization's risks. The criteria should be established by those who understand the signs early in the project that are harbingers of those risks.

## Approaches

This approach affords organizations the ability to focus on risk areas specific to their culture and to balance the lesser (but still noteworthy) risks against those that inherently pose a greater threat. Some such risk surveys will include only threat-oriented questions, while others will compare or contrast information related to opportunity as well.

In any case, the model scoring can be used to establish percentages of budget contingency or schedule contingency appropriate to the project, given its risk relative to other projects in the organization. A project scoring high in a risk model may merit a significantly higher contingency reserve than a project with relatively low risk.

### Considerations

As with any metric model, it is possible to skew the outcome by modifying the assumptions associated with the project. Thus, some model developers require that any analysis conducted is accompanied by an assumptions document that captures the environmental considerations taken into account in completing the model.

In some organizations, there have been problems with project managers who have modified the questions, the answers, the weighting scales or other components of the models. To be deployed effectively, risk models should be applied consistently from project to project. Good models will incorporate a warning as to which elements of the model are not subject to modification.

## Scope Statement

### Purpose

The scope statement may be embedded in a variety of other documents, including the project requirements document, the project charter, and the project proposal. It provides a single-statement, single-paragraph, or single-page overview of the project and its boundaries. It describes the project in clear objective terms, highlighting the outcomes and any deliverables associated with the effort. If there is a significant probability of misunderstanding, the scope statement is used to refine what is *not* included as part of the project, as well.

### Application

The scope statement may be an integral component of a variety of documents, including (but not limited to) the business case, the business justification, customer requirements, feasibility analysis, project charter, project proposal, and project request. It is used to convey a consistent vision of the project and its outcomes and to clarify project intent. In discussions about a project's goals and objectives and what should or should not be included, the scope statement often affords the defining word.

### Content

The scope statement is comprised of a clear description of the project, its outcomes, and approach:

> The project will create a new nondestructive testing methodology to validate the integrity of all on-site groove welds. The new approach may involve radiography or other technologies as appropriate, not exceeding an average cost per inspection of $3/weld. The approach will be tested and implemented no later than January 1, 2008.

This brief statement captures the nature of the work to be performed and of the work not to be performed. Expensive testing methodologies will be deemed unacceptable, but some technologies are acceptable (radiography), if they can be made appropriate in the context of the project expense. The project is for an on-site, rather than a remote, testing tool.

It could have also included the cost and budget, but some organizations do not incorporate that information because they see the scope statement as reflecting only the requirements side of the triple constraint of project management (time, cost, requirements).

### Approaches

Some scope statements will be considerably longer than others, depending on the nature of the project and the level(s) of complexity involved. The concern is that long scope statements may evolve into rudimentary requirements documents, which is generally beyond their purview. The scope statement can be used as a common frame of reference across the multiple documents that incorporate it (as described in the *Application* section).

A scope statement normally does not include a specific reference to the resources to be applied, unless they are considered a component of the actual deliverable. Identifying that 10 team members will be required to accomplish the work is not normally included in a scope statement. If the project deliverable is to include a project deliverable "authored/created/supported by John Doe," then John Doe may be identified as a resource within the scope statement, since he is actually a part of the deliverable itself.

### Considerations

The scope statement is often a highly politically charged document. Because it serves as the overarching vision for the project and provides direction for many of the other components, different constituencies may attempt to influence its development. In the ideal, these constituencies will make themselves known early in the project, so the scope statement may remain fairly static for the life of the project. While some minor modifications may be made, because of its general nature, there should not be any dramatic shifts in the verbiage within the scope statement during the life of the project.

## Stakeholder Analysis

### Purpose

In every project, there are more players than simply the buyer and the seller. Virtually all parties in the project environment have allies and foes. They have myriad "others" who take on some responsibility for the outcome of the project—either favorable or unfavorable. Because any one of these players has the potential to do harm to the project, communications at some level becomes essential for each and every stakeholder, but to communicate with them, you have to know who *they* are.

The basic premise of stakeholder analysis is one of identifying all of the key players in the project and their relative stakes. *Who has something to win or lose because of this project? What are they passionate about? What don't they care about?* Those are the rudimentary and essential questions that need to be asked of each and every stakeholder. Because projects affect change in organizations, they drive passions. People care about their outcome. As a result, they have stakes. The customer normally has a stake in improving performance or enhancing the organization's posture. The seller normally has a stake in making a profit. Individual team members' stakes may range from opportunities to deploy their skills in a challenging environment to simply marking time until they reach retirement. The difference in those stakes may drive radically different communications' needs.

Some stakeholders will want to have regular involvement in the project, with regular updates and frequent assessments of their roles and responsibilities. Others will strive to minimize their commitments, limiting the amount of project contact to the occasional e-mail update or briefing. Because of the nature of these differences, conducting a thorough stakeholder analysis is vital.

## Application

The stakeholder analysis is normally conducted by interviewing key stakeholders or conducting an e-mail survey to determine their potential role in the project, levels of interest, and potential issues they may have with the project, its deliverables or its implementation. It can take a variety of forms, but is generally documented as a precursor to the communications plan (Chapter 4) to ensure that the needs of the stakeholders will be addressed.

The form for a stakeholder analysis is normally built in a tabular format with columns delineating (at a minimum) the stakeholder names, organization, needs, and expectations (see Table 3.5 for an example). Other columns may include time frame for participation, concerns, metric assessment of the level of participation, metric assessment of the level of influence, and resources the stakeholder may be

**Table 3.5**  Sample Stakeholder Analysis

| Stakeholder Name | Division/ Organization | Area or Phase of Concern | Level of Involvement/ Participation | Primary Concerns or Issues | Needs | Expectations |
|---|---|---|---|---|---|---|
| Pat | Director, Finance Dept. | Budget | Moderate | Overruns, unreported costs | Biweekly reporting (every other Tuesday) | We will be timely and accurate in our reports. |
| Marlene | Associate, Security Dept. | Building access | Low | Unauthorized personnel | *Early* documentation of visitors, vendors | All personnel will have passes and IDs prior to their first visit. |
| Myron | Acme (CLIENT), finance | Initiation phase | High | Quality estimates for target costs | Target cost projection for CPIF contract by June 15 | Target costs will not exceed initial negotiated projections by more than 5%. |

able to engage in the project. Some suggest [9] that the stakeholder analysis should be classified according to the resources they control [1].

## Content

The source for the content in this form is a blend of experience and an environmental assessment of who will participate in the project (Table 3.5). Because the project manager or individual completing the form may have information gaps in that regard, interviews are among the most common means for extracting this information from others in the organization. Other means for data extraction include focus groups, e-mail surveys, or telephone solicitations. The project manager should ask these initial interviewees: "Who has a stake in the project's success or failure? Who should I concern myself with in assessing our approach?"

Once the initial list of potential participants has been identified, a separate round of interviews (with those individuals identified by the first group) should be conducted to complete the form.

If a column's content appears to be a subjective assessment (as with *Level of Involvement/Participation* in Table 3.5), criteria should be established for the terms used therein. Table 3.6 provides an example.

## Approaches

There are myriad ways to gather stakeholder information, but the most common approach is the face-to-face or telephone interview. A caveat in gathering information on stakeholders and stakes is that it is very easy for the interviewer to stray into requirements gathering or organizational concerns and to lose focus on the stakeholder and his or her stakes. The interview should consist of a strict effort to gather the data specifically identified on the form, radically limiting the duration of the interviews. Because a single project may have dozens or even hundreds of stakeholders, some stakeholder groups may need to be represented by a single individual.

Stakeholder analyses may also be conducted using survey forms to draw out the information. While this approach is more time effective, fewer than 100% of the intended respondents will normally respond. This may force the project manager to do extensive follow-up to ensure that the proper constituencies are identified and represented in the analysis.

## Considerations

Some stakeholders may deny or minimize their stake in the project. They may not see themselves as critical to the project's success or may not perceive their role as

**Table 3.6** Levels of Involvement Criteria

Interface with personnel on a weekly basis or more
User, creator, or assessor of project deliverables
Financially committed (internal or external)

*Low*—Meets one or none of the three criteria
*Moderate*—Meets two of the three criteria
*High*—Meets all three of the criteria

significant. That perspective can be overcome by limiting the duration of the interview to just a few minutes and by identifying the information sought before the interview occurs. Some people interpret stakeholder analysis to be more involved than it actually is.

During the life cycle of a project, the stakeholders may change as well. New participants enter and leave the project environment, and new issues and concerns create new stakes. The stakeholder analysis should be updated whenever there is a significant shift in project direction or in the makeup of the project team (both internal and external).

## Statement of Work

### Purpose

The *statement of work* (SOW) serves as a guideline of the agreements on performance between a purchasing organization and a seller of goods and/or services. It is frequently an attachment to a contract or a memorandum of understanding between two organizations. The SOW affirms how the purchasing organization wants the work to be performed and the context of that performance, including any specific management practices or protocols the contractor must follow.

### Application

The SOW is normally used as an attachment to the contract or agreement and is one of the very earliest documents developed to clarify communications between organizations. As a component of the contract, it is frequently used to settle disputes over what work should or should not be included in a project. It establishes expectations for a variety of issues in the contract relationship, including (but not limited to) the following:

- Overall project scope;
- Primary tasks and/or deliverables;
- Costs;
- Reviews and reports;
- Testing;
- Support;
- Performance requirements;
- Period of performance;
- Payments and invoicing.

Because the SOW is normally an attachment to the contract or agreement, it is a primary reference document fr the project manager throughout the life of the project.

### Content

Because the SOW is most often developed by the organization requesting the project product or service, it normally reflects a functional, rather than technical, perspective. Although the customer may have technical expertise, the work they will identify in the SOW is frequently performance oriented or performance based.

An outline for a SOW might look like the following:

## 1.0 Project Scope and Objectives

This is often a rewrite (or a copy) of the scope statement for the project, providing a general, overall perspective on what the project is intended to accomplish.

## 2.0 Description of Deliverables/Services

If the project can be defined into the key components or elements of the deliverable or service, they should be defined in sufficient detail to guide the project organization on the buyer's desired approach. This may include physical deliverables or reports, testing, and support components of the project. The description of deliverables and services is normally the single longest section of the statement of work.

## 3.0 Costs

In an internal or cost-reimbursement contract situation, a table for the anticipated costs by deliverable, month, quarter, or fiscal year may be provided. This would not be included in a firm fixed-price contract. This may include personnel and materials usage and rates, particularly in a time-and-materials contract.

## 4.0 Reviews and Reports

This is a detailed description of the regular reporting requirements associated with the project and the level of depth anticipated for those reports. It may include not only timing for the reports, but also the forms and formats required.

## 5.0 Testing

The testing component details what types of tests are considered mandatory and how and when they must be applied. This may include both formative (in-process) and summative (upon completion) evaluations.

## 6.0 Support

This component may describe support both during and immediately following the project. It should include some details about response times, type(s) of support (telephone, on site, e-mail, chat, and so forth), and what general areas may or may not be covered as a component of the support agreement.

## 7.0 Performance Requirements

If any specific organizational protocols must be followed, they should be included in the SOW. This might include security, team behavior, configuration management, risk management. and other managerial requirements of the purchasing organization.

### 8.0   Period of Performance

This should be a date-certain window of performance for the contract, from [date] to [date], with no work to be performed outside that window without a contract amendment.

### 9.0   Payment and Invoicing

This should provide specific guidance on any provisions for interim payment and identify any specific individuals responsible for ensuring payment in a timely fashion. It may also cross-reference any protocols for invoice submission.

### Approaches

In some contracting organizations, the SOW is used as a place to incorporate any special contractual clauses that may not normally be embedded in the contract. If the organization does not normally have a "furnished property" clause or other clause that may directly affect performance, such clauses are sometimes included here. In other organizations, clauses that are nestled deep within the contract, but which are often overlooked, are repeated here for emphasis. The purpose of the SOW is to clarify what work is to be performed by the project organization. If those clauses have direct influence over how the work will be performed, their inclusion here may be appropriate.

Some organizations use SOWs even for internal projects. In such environments, the SOW is used to emphasize the contractual *nature* of the relationship among the functional managers who may be responsible for the effort.

### Considerations

Project managers frequently use the SOW as virtually the sole arbiter of how they will move forward on the project. In some organizations, the SOW is the only customer-authored documentation the project manager ever sees. The project managers may not have access to the full contract, but they almost always have access to the statement of work. As the guiding force for project performance, regardless of legal consequence, the SOW is likely to be seen by the project organization as the final determinant of what the customer wants.

## System Requirements

### Purpose

System requirements provide assurance that the project's deliverables will function within a basic environment as described by the purchasing organization. Or, system requirements may be used by the project organization to describe the environment in which their deliverables will function, leaving the assurance of the environment to the purchasing organization.

### Application

System requirements are often a risk mitigation tool, applied to create a common understanding of an operational environment. A simple piece of outdoor furniture may not tolerate a tropical rain forest in the same way it would withstand a desert climate. The system requirements give all parties in the project a mental and physical framework from which to assess the potential performance characteristics of the deliverables.

## Content

The classic examples of system requirements come with every piece of software ever purchased. They describe the operating systems, computing power, and screen and graphics settings required for the software to operate properly. As such, the system requirements may include a minimum threshold, as well as a delineation of the ideal environment.

Because not all projects are related to information technology and not all information technology projects are consistent in their platform needs, some system requirements documents will be focused primarily on what the *new* system must be capable of doing. Systems requirements documents may include the following:

- *Minimum requirements.* A description of what the system must be capable of doing (buyer's perspective) or a description of what environment is required for the system to perform optimally (seller's perspective).
- *Environment.* The settings, culture, protocols, practices, or capabilities that should be in place for optimal performance by the system. This may highlight potential performance problems when the environment is less than optimal.
- *Limitations.* Certain must-have performance criteria or environments in which the system will not function at all. These criteria should be defined in detail.

## Approaches

The biggest difference in approach to the system requirements depends on authorship. If the system requirements are written by the buyer, then they will reflect the purchaser's environment, culture, and conditions. If the requirements are crafted by the seller, they will reveal the seller's capabilities in different environments and will provide definition on what environments are optimal for their standard deliverables.

## Considerations

Some organizations use the system requirements as a fail-safe to protect against organizations that will not comply with their environment. Organizations that are driven by graphics, for example, often use the "must function on MacIntosh" system requirement to ensure that all of their heavily graphics-oriented personnel will be able to access the products of the deliverable. Because the system requirements may include such diverse elements as temperature, humidity, computer speed, dust, noise levels, and ambient light, the requirements sometimes become a fail-safe for the authors, who can blame the environmental conditions, rather than the project or supporting organization for any performance shortcomings.

## Conclusion

No organization will use all of these documents in the initial phases of their projects, but they will use a wide enough array that the project manager should have a clear sense of what the documents should incorporate. Many organizations take standard practices and modify them to meet organizationally specific needs. The key is to be able to achieve a common understanding of what the documents, protocols, and practices are designed to accomplish and to ensure that they accomplish those goals.

## References

[1]    *Guide to the Project Management Body of Knowledge,* Newton Square, PA, Project Management Institute, 2000.

[2]    Bullard, T. M., "Proactive Intervention: Identifying and Resolving Issues with Problem Projects before they Become Problems," *Proc. PMI Seminar,* San Antonio, TX, 2002.

[3]    Cooper, M., "Contingency When Approaching IT Service Projects," *Proc. PMI Seminar,* San Antonio, TX, 2002.

[4]    Suffredini, M., *Window Operational Research Facility Project Requirements Document,* International Space Station Program, Houston, TX: National Aeronautics and Space Administration, 1999.

[5]    Malcolm Baldrige National Quality Improvement Act of 1987.

[6]    *NASA Goddard Space Flight Center Quality Policy Statement,* http://seawifs.gsfc.nasa.gov/SEAWIFS/ISO/, updated February 25, 2000.

[7]    *DLS Quality Policy Statement,* http://www.chppmeur.healthcare.hqusareur.army.mil/departments/dls/dls_quality_policy.htm.

[8]    Carr, M., et al., *Taxonomy-Based Risk Identification,* Pittsburgh, Software Engineering Institute, Carnegie Mellon University, 1993.

[9]    Brinkerhoff, D. W., *Improving Development Program Performance,* Boulder, CO: Lynne Reinner Publishers, 1991.

## CHAPTER 4

# Communications Tools in the Planning Processes

Project plans ultimately manifest themselves as deliverables. As such, the communications tools applied here reflect the need to express a clear understanding of both the intent of the project and the deliverables that are to be produced. These are largely the "road maps" for the project, communicating information on how to get from one point in the project to a point closer to the final project objective. Many of these tools are specific components of the project plan (see later section), which is the larger, overarching document that serves as a repository for a host of subplans.

## Blueprints/Schematics

### Purpose

The classic blue blueprint actually stems from an old copying technique whereby copies were made by passing light through a drawing done on tracing paper. The chemical composition of the copy paper when struck by light turned most of the paper blue, while the area not exposed remained white [1]. The term *blueprint* has now come to mean any detailed drawing or rendering. The modern technical equivalent would be the schematic drawing. Blueprints and schematics are used to provide consistent guidance on what the final deliverable should look like, including dimensions, relative size, and configuration.

### Application

Classically used in the construction industry, blueprints have become a standard of product development organizations, as well. Blueprints and schematics are used (as they were historically) to provide multiple copies of a consistent document reflecting the desired outcome of the project. They are used by both the buyer and seller to ensure that they speak a common language in terms of their understanding of what the final outcome of the project should look like.

### Content

The common characteristics of blueprints are that they have a scale for the size of the deliverables, as well as clear indications of the dimensions of any component elements displayed in the drawing. For schematics, the scale may not be exact, but the types of components to be used and the nature of those components will be expressed in detail. Both have legends that describe any unusual symbols that are used to represent features in the drawing. In electrical contracting, for example, the letter *S* or a dollar sign ($) on the drawing represents an electrical switch. The blueprint normally spans as many pages as are necessary to capture renderings of the project deliverable from multiple angles and at different levels of depth or detail. The schematic may also span multiple pages, but the varied angles are generally not required. Particularly complex elements may be given their own page or an inset drawing to highlight the complexities.

All of the drawings will have measurements to clarify the dimensions of the deliverables and may incorporate environmental considerations (such as elevation or installation environment) as components of the drawing. Cross sections are not uncommon, particularly when it is important to illustrate the differences among deliverables that might look the same externally.

### Approaches

Classic white-on-blue blueprints have become far less common over the years, particularly with the advent of *computer-assisted design* (CAD) programs. More often, blueprints and schematics are now conventional black-and-white drawings rendered on a computer plotter and modified on-line with the contractor. Because blueprint practices have been adopted by product developers and other nonconstruction industries, levels of detail now may be measured in millimeters and microns, rather than feet and meters. The basic principles remain the same, however. Both the blueprint and schematic provide a common understanding of the ultimate look of the deliverable.

### Considerations

Because they are sometimes reviewed by those unfamiliar with the trades responsible for the construction, the customer should be educated regarding any elements that may be misleading or misconstrued. (For instance, the dollar sign mentioned earlier that represents the light switch could have a double meaning to the individual paying the bills.) For blueprints or schematics of an extremely technical nature (e.g., computer chips), customer education will be essential, particularly for elements of the design that are considered leading edge.

## Budgets

### Purpose

Budgets provide a categorized breakdown of anticipated project costs. They define, by area, anticipated costs (including any pass-through, mark-up, contingency, or administrative percentages). The cost breakdowns are available for individual elements and are subtotaled by category and totaled for the project as a whole. When authorized, budgets serve as the organization's expectation for project spending.

### Application

In most organizations, budgets are established so that funds may be properly allocated to a project. Although they are defined here as planning tools, they may be used during the initiation process in certain organizations where only well-defined cost plans are used in making the project go/no-go decision. They serve as a spending baseline, to determine when project costs are or are not within the anticipated boundaries for spending.

Depending on organizational preference, the budget line items may be broad in scope (with a heading like "Resources") or extremely detailed (with individual human and material resources, identified by name). The budget is decomposed to the degree necessary for the organization to effectively use the information, and to the degree where the information's accuracy may ultimately be reconciled with actual costs at project completion.

These actual costs normally include a percentage to acknowledge the organization's investment and expense in administering a project. This burden rate may be different for human and material resources, depending upon the organization's accounting practices. Normally, budget costs are broken out by resources and materials so that the burden for each can be easily incorporated and so that management can discern between human resource costs and material resource costs.

## Content

Because the components of project budgets are highly specialized (based on the nature and type of work being performed), their "standardized" content is limited. A budget incorporating some of the more common elements might be formatted as shown in Table 4.1.

**Table 4.1**   Budget Planning Form

| Direct | Units Required | Cost/Unit | Total |
|---|---|---|---|
| Labor | | | |
| ☐ Resource Class #1 | | | |
| ☐ Resource Class #2 | | | |
| ☐ Resource Class #3 | | | |
| Labor Burden | | | |
|   Subtotal | | | |
| Materials | | | |
| ☐ Hardware | | | |
| ☐ Software | | | |
| Materials Burden | | | |
|   Subtotal | | | |
| Travel | | | |
| Outreach/marketing | | | |
| Legal | | | |
| Shipping | | | |
| Contractors/brokers | | | |
| Fees | | | |
| Transport | | | |
| Other | | | |
|   Subtotal | | | |
| G&A | | | |
| Reserve | | | |
| Total | | | |

The key is to adapt the budget and its forms and formats to the needs of the organization and the specific nature of the project in question.

### Approaches

Some budgets are generated only at a very high level (with virtually no detail) because the information available early in the project planning stages is scant. Others break down the hours committed on a per-resource basis rooted in the resources committed at the work package level of the work breakdown structure. In either case, the depth of the budget should be acceptable to senior management, because their authorization is required to convert budget predictions into organizational allocations of funds.

### Considerations

Although project budget allocations may change as project requirements shift, the original budget baseline should be retained for the life of the project as an historic artifact. Regardless of the number of changes which are approved, the original budget remains significant in that it is normally the only financial allocation tool that receives the approval of the highest levels of management.

In some organizations, budget figures are arbitrarily adjusted by senior management, under the assumption that there is an inherent level of unauthorized reserve or "fudge" nestled within the numbers. Such arbitrary downward adjustments contribute to an ongoing cycle of inaccuracy, as team members learn to anticipate the management adjustments and modify their estimates accordingly.

Sharing budget information with management and the team may depend largely on organizational protocols, but unless there are overriding reasons, budget information may be shared openly with the team. Some organizations advocate "open book" management, which means that budget information is readily available to team members in a secure internal environment. If the information is to be made readily available to team members in such an environment, consistent forms and formats become crucial to ensure consistent interpretations of the data.

## Change Control Plan

### Purpose

The change control plan allows project managers to affirm organizational protocols for change and to assert project-specific change control practices and policies in an effort to more effectively manage project modifications. It serves as the common process for all changes, and assets when changes may be deemed as formally "accepted."

### Application

The change control plan is established either independently or with the support of the *project management office* (PMO) or *project support office* (PSO). It is provided to all project stakeholders who may either have an interest in changing the project or be affected by such a change. It is used to gain consensus on how and when changes will be implemented (or rejected).

## Content

The change control plan should identify organizationally standard change process information, as well as information specific to the project. It should account for a variety of stakeholders, including team members, customers, management, project office personnel, end users, and the project manager. As such, the change control plan has a far reach and can cross-reference a number of other change-related documents.

The change control plan may have an outline similar to that discussed in the following subsections.

### 1.0   Rationale

The rationale for the change process should be clearly explained, because some personnel are likely to see change control protocols as an unnecessary administrative layer. The rationale should explain that the plan incorporates both internal and external change, and it should identify the key players in the change process.

### 2.0   Process

The single longest component of the change control plan, the process should clearly identify how change is initiated, the sources of change, where change requests or change notices are directed, and the administrative procedures for tracking and following up on the change of approved requirements. There may be numerous cross-references to other documents, including change control forms and a change request log.

*2.1   Background*   The project-specific background information should be provided, identifying key personnel and their roles and any regulatory agencies with project oversight responsibility.

*2.2   Change Initiation*   For all changes, some initial sorting function must be done to determine the scope of the change, the level of responsibility for approvals and/or acceptance, and the procedures for notification.

*2.3   Change Documentation*   Normally, basic change documentation comes in the form of a change request form or a change control form. The latter may be more appropriate in dealing with changes driven by the environment (technical or natural), rather than by a specific "request" from a project stakeholder.

*2.4   Change Process Flow*   Often in the form of a flow diagram, the flow may illustrate how different levels of change are managed, such as when cost or schedule thresholds are exceeded or when the change might require the approval or acceptance of a regulatory or executive authority. A sample flow diagram is shown in Figure 4.1.

*2.5   Tracking*   Any long-term tracking or monitoring processes should be clearly identified and should, again, cross-reference other documents required specifically to

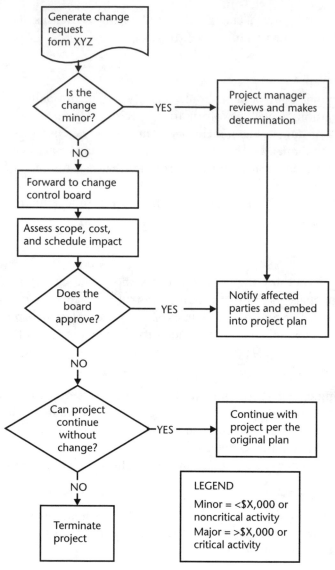

**Figure 4.1** Change process.

track or monitor the ongoing success of a change implementation. Specifically, any procedures for regular monitoring of change status should be identified here. This section should also capture any protocols for expressing information for lessons learned or process improvement associated with the change.

*2.6 Approvals*    The names, roles, or levels of any approval authorities required for any level of change implementation should be clearly identified. The level of their authority should be clarified as well.

## 3.0  Attachments

The attachments to a change control plan often include change control forms, any process documentation, a roster of members for the change control board (if applicable), and a change request log. Ideally, all of the change-related information should be available in a common repository, and the attachments section of the plan often becomes that repository.

### 4.0 Signatures

The change control plan should be signed and approved by those parties directly affected.

### Approaches

Because some organizations do not favor a document-rich change control process, the change control plan may be a simple guide on who to turn to in the event of a proposed change. Because other organizations may be engaged in intense configuration management, the change control plan may have numerous extensive cross-references to detailed processes and subprocesses for implementing even the most seemingly benign of changes. The details of the change control plan should be a direct reflection of the level of rigor of the organization's change control practices.

### Considerations

Change control plans are politically charged, because they put the project manager in an enforcement role. As such, the more that can be done to achieve early buy-in on the change control plan, the forms, and the processes, the less pressure the project manager will be under to serve as the "change police." The change control plan should set expectations for team members, customers, and management and should be applied even when the changes are perceived as no-cost or low-cost changes. Through consistent application, the change control plan can become a calming force even in the most volatile projects.

# Communications Plan

### Purpose

The communications plan provides direction on which stakeholders should be discussing project business with which other stakeholders, the tools they should use, and the degree to which they should be sharing, documenting, and storing that information. Because of the number of stakeholders involved in a single project and their diverse roles, the communications plan orchestrates project communication through a cohesive approach to information sharing. It is a critical deliverable to the planning process.

### Application

The communications plan is shared openly with all internal project stakeholders to help them understand how they should communicate and with whom. For external project stakeholders, the communications plan is normally filtered to present information *only* germane to their role and use.

Ideally, the list should be built in a spreadsheet program that allows the user to filter stakeholders by communications modes, contacts, frequency, or other category as appropriate.

The communications plan should reflect communications as dictated by the contract, memorandum of understanding, or statement of work, as well as any other protocols that became self-evident during the project's evolution. Different project participants will use the communications plan in different ways:

- The project manager uses the communications plan to ensure that the various stakeholders are aware of their communications responsibilities to each other and to the organizations.
- Team members use the communications plan as a combination contact list and guide, with an interest in the types of communication preferred by the various users.
- Senior management and customers may use an abridged version of the communications plan to be clear on when to expect certain reports and documentation, and for contact information on their primary points of contact.

## Content

The communications plan is a matrix of information, normally built in a spreadsheet program with the following data:

- Stakeholder name;
- Primary contact;
- Secondary contact;
- Telephone;
- E-mail;
- Postal mail address;
- Preferred communications mode;
- Best time;
- Frequency of communication.

Because it is built in a spreadsheet format, the communications plan can be sorted and reordered in a variety of ways. If the types of communication (status reports, team meetings) are most important, they may be the first column, followed by frequency of communication and stakeholders (recipients and attendees, respectively). If physical proximity is an issue, the primary consideration may be the postal mail address, which can be sorted to determine which stakeholders are in common regions or locales.

Because communications breakdowns are frequently rooted not in miscommunication, but by a lack of communication, the notion of the "best time" for meetings, reports, contacts, and phone calls is crucial. If certain team members can only attend project meetings before 3 p.m. because of personal concerns, the project communications plan should highlight those interests. If a customer is never available before 10 a.m. for phone calls, such concerns should be noted as well.

### Approaches

The communications plan is one of the most publicly available of the project documents. Because it serves as the framework for open communication among team members, the customer, and other stakeholders, complete and abridged versions of the document may exist, depending on the audience. If varying versions are used, some form of version control (e.g., 1.0 = complete plan, 1.1 = customer abridged, 1.2 = management abridged) should be applied.

The communications plan serves as more than just a phone directory. It provides information on the communications sensibilities and sensitivities of all of the personnel involve.

### Considerations

While the plan is widely available, some stakeholders are proprietary about their contact information, and those concerns need to be respected. The communications plan should not become a medium for those who wish to broadcast information randomly to all project parties. It should be used to focus communications on an as-needed basis.

## Comprehensive Test Plan

### Purpose

Whether for software, hardware, or process, a comprehensive test plan, as the name implies, is designed to guide an exhaustive test of the system in question. It identifies the potential areas of risk and explains how the system will be evaluated to determine its susceptibility to problems. The test plan also delineates how the test results will be validated. As test results are received, they are amended to the test plan so the process and its results can be evaluated *in toto*.

### Application

Because a comprehensive test plan expresses a process to be used and then, later, is married to the results of that process, it is an evolutionary document. It grows as the available information grows. Initially, the comprehensive test plan serves as a road map for test conduct and validation. Later, it serves as a repository for the outputs of the tests, as well. As such the document is essential to those who will be conducting the tests and may be used as a defense for the costs of the tests or the approach.

### Content

A comprehensive test plan includes a history and step-by-step process guidance for the evaluation.

*Background.*    The rationale for the tests is normally the first component of a comprehensive test plan, explaining why the tests were deemed necessary and what environmental considerations led to the primary approach(es) being considered.

*Testing approach.*     The actual technical approach to the testing should be defined in detail, including any materials required, the range of parameters the test will evaluate, specific areas to be tested, and indicators or metrics to be tracked. In addition, this may include testing of individual components of the system, as well as integrated systems.

*Validation.*     Any validation processes, whether internal or independent, should be defined as objectively as possible. The validation processes should address the specific components being tested, as well as any integrated systems.

*Outcomes anticipated.*     Some test plans (not all) will include some explanations of the outputs anticipated from the testing process, so the anticipated outcomes can be compared with the actual outcomes. This should not be used to guide the testing outcomes, but should be used to identify if the testing process spelled out in the plan will actually produce outcomes of the type desired.

*Outcomes tested.*     As stated earlier, the test plan is evolutionary. This information will only be incorporated after the testing is completed. This information may be incorporated in stages as preliminary and final testing may span several weeks, months, or years.

*Conclusion(s).*     Based on the tested, validated outcomes, any conclusions that can be drawn based on the system, the testing process, the validation, and the anticipated outcomes should be expressed as conclusions. The conclusions should be part of the comprehensive test plan for the organizational archive.

## Approach

Unlike other documentation where there may be heavier and lighter versions of the documentation, the comprehensive test plan is, by its nature, as exhaustive as possible. Every element of information that can be included in the test plan should be included to preclude misunderstanding or misapplication of the testing process. Also, while some plans by their nature incorporate some measure of variability, that does not apply with a test plan. Test plans are relatively rigid, and if the process is to be changed, the test plan documentation should be changed as well.

## Considerations

The comprehensive test plan can apply to materials, systems, processes, hardware and software, or integrated systems thereof. For some of those tests, the results are purely quantitative, and variance is easily detected. For processes, however, testing can become speculative if the outputs of the process are not clearly identified in a way that can be objectively measured. Subjective measurement leads to inadequate testing, as the "hard" metrics are lost. If no concrete measures can be found for a process testing evaluation or validation, such shortcomings should be highlighted in the test plan, so the results are not misconstrued as hard fact.

## Cost Baseline

### Purpose

The cost baseline is a real or theoretical construct that captures the approved budget distributed over time. It is used to provide a comparison or contrast with the actual costs and their application over time. The cost baseline is used to determine if performance to date is within acceptable parameters.

### Application

The baseline is normally maintained with other project information in either project management or spreadsheet software. It is used both for comparison and reporting and is normally a critical element in project status reports, progress reports, and forecasts. The cost baseline serves as affirmation of what the project's cost structure looked like when the project was originally approved. According to the Project Management Institute, the cost baseline incorporates any approved changes.

The cost baseline is developed by aggregating the costs of the individual work elements and then combining them at time (or work) intervals where meaningful actual cost information will be available.

### Content

The cost baseline includes work element-by-work element, time unit-by-time unit detail depicted across the timeline. One of the most common depictions of the cost baseline is the expenditure of funds shown in a cumulative cost curve like that of Figure 4.2.

The cost baseline can also simply be a work breakdown structure with an additional column for the baseline costs of each work package.

### Approach

Because cost information comes in a variety of formats and can be displayed in the context of time or work, the formats for the cost baseline are legion. While the

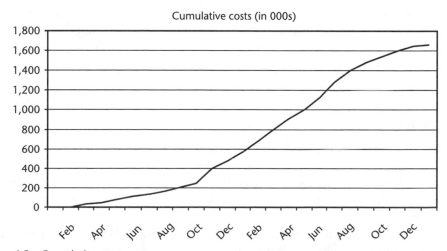

**Figure 4.2** Cumulative cost curve.

cumulative cost curve is among the most common, spreadsheets comparing work and the investment for that work are also relatively commonplace. For *all* costs in the cumulative cost curve, however, the funds should be those that the funding organization recognizes as the agreed-on funding allocations for the project.

### Considerations

Baselines are not malleable. They do not change with the vagaries of project life. While changes should be reflected *with* the baseline, the original baseline should remain intact. The only time a baseline should change is when it is rendered meaningless by the sheer volume of changes (either planned or unplanned). Because the baseline serves as the primary metric for evaluating performance as the project progresses, the stability of the baseline is crucial. Because it is such a critical metric, communicating it to the team through open book budgets, regular e-mail communications, or as a component of the project plan is vital to ensuring a consistent understanding of the budget.

## Data Flow Diagrams

### Purpose

The purpose of a data flow diagram is to highlight and illustrate where data come from. It is most distinguishable by what it is not. It is not designed to highlight or illustrate data flow and sequence; it is instead intended simply to capture the essence of what data are where and how they may be retrieved.

### Application

The data flow diagram is used in determining what information is available in any given process or system and where the information may come from. It can be used in any effort where data gathering is critical to project success and where data come from multiple sources to contribute to a greater whole.

It is often a component of process diagramming, particularly where new processes are being considered and where data from a variety of sources and systems will be deployed in a new fashion. Classic examples include information integration systems such as resource management and logistics systems, as well as any system that draws on customer information (or any information being drawn from multiple sources).

### Content

The content is a diagram that depicts data titles as circles with arrows pointing toward their new "home" or process repository. For some data, it must flow through multiple repositories before the diagram is complete. Again, the diagram is not intended to illustrate process, but simply the channels through which data must flow.

The simple example in Figure 4.3 illustrates a *data flow diagram* (DFD) for an updated telephone directory listing.

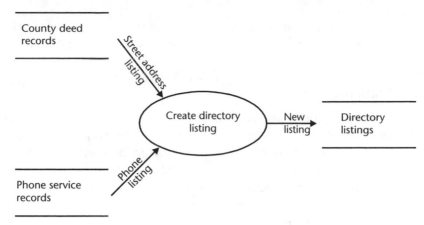

**Figure 4.3** Data flow diagram.

By its nature, the DFD will include components of processes and process steps (represented by ovals), data repositories (represented by parallel lines), and external forces that may interact with the process (represented by rectangles). Arrows highlight data flow, and while that may appear to be a process step, a DFD does not inherently reflect sequence. In the example shown in Figure 4.3, it is possible that *all* of the county deeds are reviewed, recorded, and stored before the telephone company records are reviewed. Because they both feed the same node does not imply that they are concurrent.

### Approaches

Some individuals try to blend the data flow diagram with process diagrams. That is not the true intent of a data flow diagram. The DFD is designed to extract information about where the data are stored and where one may go to gain access to them. It is a tool with a single, simple purpose—identify the sources of data.

### Considerations

In building data flow diagrams, team members may naturally stumble across information regarding process flow and process interaction. Although that is not the province of the DFD, it is information that may prove valuable as the effort proceeds. Thus, the facilitator responsible for the DFD may want to record and catalog process information discovered during the DFD development process for later analysis and for incorporation into process flow diagrams or workflow diagrams.

## Design Specifications

### Purpose

Design specifications, like blueprints, provide detailed guidance on what the project outputs will look like and how they will be expected to perform. The key difference is that design specifications provide that guidance through the written word, coupled with graphics and drawings, whereas blueprints are strictly graphic in nature.

The purpose is to provide clear direction to the project organization on what the final outputs of the project must look like and the tolerances and standards those outputs must meet.

## Application

Design specifications are used as soon as they are available to determine some components of the work to be performed and to prepare for the purchasing and allocation of materials to the project. Because design specifications incorporate information about certain performance standards, the specifications can even be helpful in determining which resources are best suited to assist in or perform some of the work, because some work requires more highly specialized workers than others. The design specifications are used to flesh out the customers' functional requirements *and* technical requirements, expressing specifically how those needs will be addressed by the look and feel of the final deliverables. The components of the design specification should be traceable back to the functional and technical requirements, and there should be evidence that each component of the design specification will be addressed by some component of the work breakdown structure.

In deliverables-oriented organizations (in contrast to service organizations), the design specifications often become the document used to define project intent, expectations, and commitments. They are often referenced in project litigation as the rationale for certain approaches.

## Content

As with many project documents, the differences in design specifications may vary widely with the type of project being created. Since the design specifications are often the most detailed of the project documents, they can span dozens of pages (or even volumes) in larger projects. The common elements of design specifications are discussed in the following subsections.

### 1.0   Introduction/Overview

This normally consists of the scope statement for the project, coupled with any references to outside documentation or sources. If certain standards or protocols common to the industry must be applied, this is where they would be identified as well.

### 2.0   Performance Criteria

Drawn from the technical and functional requirements, the design specifications highlight what performance criteria must be met. If the criteria can be supported by drawings or graphic representations, those are incorporated here as well. As with most of the design specifications document, cross-references to external sources should be included here, as appropriate.

### 3.0   Design Requirements

Often the longest component of the document, the design requirements provide specific detail on what the project outputs will look, feel, and operate like. They will define what needs must be served in a variety of areas, from appearance to test performance. Any special characteristics that must be present in the final deliverables are delineated here.

## 4.0   Components

While the material components of a project deliverable are frequently called out in the design requirements, some design specifications will incorporate a separate heading to ensure that there is no ambiguity on how those components must function and what parameters they must meet.

## 5.0   Glossary of Terms

Because design specifications are highly specialized and technical documents, a glossary of terms affords a consistent application of the technical language.

### Approaches

In deliverables-oriented organizations, design specifications are sometimes referred to as *detailed* design specifications. That reinforces the perspective that these documents provide extensive detail. In some organizations, team members may strive to intentionally omit certain details from the design specifications in order to allow greater flexibility in design. This is not uncommon in the software industry, but is not a best practice in project management. The more detail that can be afforded the team in terms of how the customer needs can best be served by the project, the higher the likelihood of success.

### Considerations

Design specifications have their roots in industry where physical deliverables are produced. As such, the orientation with design specifications is to provide physical descriptions of objects, components, and all aspects of the deliverable. Design specifications can still be employed on service projects, however. By defining how processes should perform and graphically representing any specific needs of the customer organization, the same processes that have served product industries for decades can be applied in those organizations providing services, rather than products.

# Development Plan: Personal/Individual

## Purpose

Individual development plans are designed to provide a clear vision as to the individual competencies and capabilities that a team member hopes to develop during the course of a given time period or project. The plan is used by management to ensure that the employee is taking clear steps toward specific professional goals and objectives. It is used by team members as a guide or reminder of specific activities they intend to pursue.

## Application

The individual development plan is generally applied at a career landmark, either an annual review or the beginning of a new set of roles and responsibilities. At the beginning of a project, the individual development plan provides insight on how the project will benefit the team member, rather than the other way around. It gives both team members and managers a clear understanding of what specific competencies will evolve during the project life cycle.

The plan is normally used at the beginning of the team member's participation in the project and is reviewed on a regular schedule. It should reflect the goals or competencies to be achieved, the means to achieve them, and the time frame in which they will be achieved. Depending on the organization, the costs associated with any professional development may be documented here as well.

## Content

The personal development plan will include both general statements regarding goals and objectives, as well as specific behaviors aimed at achieving those objectives.

### 1.0   Competencies/Objectives

The competencies or objectives are those capabilities that either the team member or management or both have determined are appropriate and critical to personal and professional growth. The appropriate competencies may be determined by extended study or analysis (as in the Defense Systems Management College's Program Manager Competency Model, created in 1989) or by virtue of organizational need or individual professional curiosity and zeal.

### 2.0   Activities

The activities are those developmental activities (training, cross-training, research, and so on) that provide guidance in the competencies. The specific objectives of the activities should reflect the objectives as described in Section 1.0.

### 3.0   Timing

Either a window of time or a "no-later-than" date is documented for each activity. This ensures a common understanding of the relative urgency of the competency or objective and a sense of the development's relative value to other activities.

### 4.0   Cost

Some organizations need to have a cost structure for individual development programs to determine if they are getting a sufficient return for their investment. The costs may be documented in monetary values, individual resource hours, or both.

## Approaches

The development plan may evolve through an iterative approach, if the organization wants to engage the team member in its creation. In some cases, the team members will identify specific professional goals and then compare their personal objectives with those of their management. If the two are reasonably close, the team member's approach may be adopted. If there is some distance between the two visions, the team member's perspectives may be incorporated with those of management to create a list of mutually accepted competencies or objectives.

Ideally, it should be possible to document what progress is being made toward competency development at regular intervals. Because the objectives are clearly stated, any progress toward their accomplishment should be easy to identify.

### Considerations

Development plans can be powerful tools if they are achievable and well designed. Good development plans will have some objectives that can be achieved in a relatively short (2- to 4-month) time span. Other objectives may take years to achieve. A balance should be struck between the different classes of objectives.

The objectives may be tied to incentives, financial and otherwise. If they are, the incentives should be clearly delineated with the competencies, but care should be taken to avoid providing incentives only for those objectives achieved by a certain date. Performance objectives should add value whenever they occur within an individual's career.

## Development Plan: Strategic

### Purpose

This narrative discussion is a defense for a particular perspective on how or why an organization should move in a particular strategic direction in terms of developing new business, new markets, new facilities, or new resources. Strategic development plans outline the vision for how those new components would be integrated into the traditional organizational practice. They also delineate how the approach serves the organization's vision.

### Application

Strategic development plans are a component of presentations to stakeholders on how and or why they should endorse the vision as outlined. The plans are used as the foundation for implementing new projects related to the new business, markets, facilities, or resources.

### Content

A strategic development plan includes information on the current state of the organization, the proposed changes, the envisioned outcome, and the relationship of the change to the organization's overarching strategies and visions. As a narrative discussion, the information may be presented in virtually any sequence, but the key is to ensure that clear relationships are drawn between the change and the organizational strategy.

The plan includes a high-level, step-by-step outline of how the development plan will be implemented and how the changes will be phased in.

### Approaches

As a plan, the level of detail will vary depending on the amount of information available and the progress that has already been achieved toward the goals. The more information that is available (and the greater the level of involvement of the document's audience), the more detail that may be offered in the development plan.

### Considerations

Because there are different types of strategic development plans (markets, facilities, resources, and so on), there will be differences in emphasis. The key is to select an area of emphasis and to keep the document focused on that area. A key failing in strategic development plans is that they sometimes become overly ambitious, attempting to address too many strategic areas concurrently.

## Document Control Plan

### Purpose

The document control plan is an outline or guide on how physical or virtual documents will be managed throughout the life of the project. It provides a road map for tracking documents and for adding, archiving, and removing new documentation from the process.

### Application

The document control plan is used whenever sufficient documentation exists to warrant a specific process for the control, sequencing, and maintenance of documentation through multiple channels. It is initiated to ensure that those involved with the project share an understanding of how information in the project will be managed and who will have access to which documentation at which point in time. It is used during the project as both affirmation of the process and as the means to educate others on the process application.

### Content

A document control plan may consist of little more than an index of available documentation and its intended locations, or, in more ornate applications, it may consist of a matrix of documents and their owners, locations, update schedules, circulation lists, archival locations, and destruction dates, as shown in Table 4.2.

In the examples shown in Table 4.2, some of the common issues with document control are evident. Depending on how the document is crafted, it may be necessary to update the document control document any time a document is updated. Such would be the case with the "Location" column as crafted, because each document is called out in its most current version. By contrast, if a wildcard location is called out (as in the "Archive" column), then the document control plan may go for a more extended period without an update. Similarly, if team and organizational titles are identified, rather than names, the need for frequent updates may be lessened significantly.

### Approaches

The document control plan can be approached in a variety of ways, including straight narrative or the tabular format shown here. There are normally extensive

**Table 4.2**  Sample Document Control Plan

|  | Owner | Location | Update Schedule | Circulation | Archive | Destruction |
|---|---|---|---|---|---|---|
| Document Name | Name of the responsible party | Physical or virtual location of current version | Frequency of updates | Names or functions of applicable stakeholders | Physical or virtual location of past versions | Maintenance schedule or final destruction date |
| *Examples* | | | | | | |
| Stakeholder list | Project manager | M:/Project a/Mas-Doc/Stakelist.0 7.doc | First team meeting each month | Project team | M:/Project a/Arc-Doc/Stakelist.*.* | Project sign-off date, plus 3 years |
| WBS | Project manager | M:/Project a/Mas-Doc/ProjA.05. mpp | Every 6 weeks | PM, assistant PM, team, Jeff Zohnd | M:/Project a/MasDoc/ ProjΛ.*.*.mpp | Project sign-off date, plus 5 years |
| Team charter | Team representative (Mark Lamoncha) | M:/Project a/Mas-Doc/Team Agree.02. doc | Whenever new team members are added | Project team | M:/Project a/MasDoc/ Team Agree.*.*.doc | Project sign-off date, plus 6 months |

cross-references to other documentation and to storage repositories within the organization. Document control frequently incorporates the protocols for version control of documentation as well. This may be as simple as incrementally renaming files as new iterations are created (e.g., Document01, Document02, Document03) or may involve protocols that address authorship, ownership, or the responsible party for the latest iterations (e.g., Document01.Bob03, Document01.Bob03-Martin01). The rationale for and description of the approach(es) should be clearly delineated in the narrative associated with the document control plan.

### Considerations

While project managers may be tempted to arbitrarily set the archive and destruction dates for aging documents, the legal aspects of document maintenance need to be considered. Project organizations have legal responsibilities to their clients and to their governments and regulators to maintain certain documents. The laws regarding document retention vary from region to region and agency to agency. Before establishing (and implementing) document destruction protocols, legal counsel should be sought.

## Goals and Objectives

### Purpose

Goals and objectives provide uniform direction on a project and ensure a consistent vision across the body of stakeholders. Ideally, the goals and objectives serve as a consistent reference for decision making related to the project.

## Application

Goals and objectives are publicly available information elements that are normally shared either through meeting documentation or as introductory information in project plans and other project support documentation. The goals and objectives are used to unify the vision of the team and the organization regarding what the project is to accomplish and the general approach to accomplishing that goal. They may be posted in a highly visible location to ensure that they are readily available to all team members. Management theorist Peter Drucker [2] suggests that the goals of a business should drive its specific work objectives, and that those objectives need to be delineated clearly to ensure higher levels of performance.

## Content

Goals and objectives should clearly state the intent of the organization, the project, and the tasks or effort under consideration—and the objectives of individual workers in the organization should be complementary in serving the goal. Goal statements are set at a high level, describing what the organization hopes to achieve. They are closely tied to vision statements in that the goals are descriptions of what the organization hopes to accomplish. Goals can be constructed at the organizational level (e.g., "To become a recognized software innovator by changing how software is designed and supported") or at a more detailed, project level (e.g., "To provide Acme with innovative logistics software that supports their inventory tracking and maintenance"). In either case, the goals are general statements that are supported by objectives.

Objectives serve the goal. They provide clear, unambiguous direction on how the goals will be met. Ideally, they should be sufficiently clear that they allow for self-control and self-monitoring by the team members to whom they are given [2], which means that each objective should have some metric form of measurement that reflects the organization's values. If the goal is to provide innovative logistics software to support Acme, the objectives might include the following:

- To provide a system that provides real-time information regarding material location, storage, and aging;
- To provide a system that responds with customized (detailed, step-by-step) direction on alternative sources for material that is out of stock or in low supply.

Terms become important in establishing goals and objectives. The assumption that anything that may be misinterpreted will be misinterpreted is a fair and reasonable assumption. One person's vision of "low supply" might be different than another's. The effort in building objectives is to minimize the ambiguity as much as is possible and reasonable.

## Approaches

A blurry line exists between goals and objectives and between objectives and requirements. As such, one person's general "goal" statement might be sufficiently detailed to be an objective for someone else (particularly someone at a higher level in the organization). Because objectives should be rendered as clearly as possible, the effort to build in the appropriate level of detail sometimes generates the nascent requirements.

To construct better goals and objectives, goals should address the future state of the project, deliverable, or organization. Objectives should state how the team and the project will work in that direction.

In some organizations, the objective statement is always linked to specific time and cost limitations.

### Considerations

Because goals and objectives provide direction, they should be public pronouncements. In meetings and in project facilities, the objectives and goals of a project should be clearly posted to ensure team familiarity with the documentation. Such openness about the goals and objectives can preclude some of the inherent squabbling sometimes evident when project team members seem to be working at cross purposes.

Such visibility should also be accompanied by encouragement of team members to identify any effort that does not seem to be clearly serving the project goals. If some work serves the project goals indirectly, it is important to clarify how that work will ultimately serve the project purposes, so the team members working on those functions will understand their role in the project as a whole.

## Help Desk Procedures

### Purpose

Help desk procedures are designed to provide help desk personnel with a step-by-step review of virtually every possible permutation of problems they may encounter with end users while serving on a help desk. such procedures may not seem project oriented, but they do provide a great deal of insight into how to establish any step-by-step, decision-by-decision protocol a project or its output might require.

### Application

Help desk procedures are used in environments where individuals providing customer service or support may have limited knowledge of or experience with the systems for which they are providing support. But help desk procedures presuppose that those providing the service do have a great deal of general knowledge and the ability to draw analogies from that general knowledge into the specifics of the help desk environment. The procedures provide them with the specifics required to address the narrow focus of individualized problems.

### Content

Because the help desk procedures must cover a host of eventualities, they tend to be rather voluminous, spanning dozens of pages, even for the most rudimentary systems. They will have some common elements, including these:

- Procedures for Documenting the Help Request (Request Initiation)
  - Name of requester (including contact information);
  - System/project for which help is requested (including platforms/ environment);
  - Nature of the help request (type of request and specifics);
  - Most recent dispensation/status/prioritization.
- Procedures for Troubleshooting the Request
  - Most common concerns;
  - Troubleshooting questions and answers;
  - Secondary concerns;
  - Standard solutions;
  - Secondary solutions;
  - Alternative information sources;
  - Escalation procedures.
- Administrative Follow-Up
  - Time spent;
  - Resolution (standard/new);
  - Rationale;
  - Lessons learned (documentation of new solutions);
  - Status;
  - Follow-up required.

## Approaches

Some organizations use procedures as a means to "dummy-proof" their systems, by providing such extensive support and detail that every possible eventuality (theoretically) has been considered. Such efforts are challenging to support, in that system changes and environmental changes may generate new conditions that had not previously been considered. The antithesis of that approach is to provide only general and administrative guidance, assuming that the help desk support personnel will have the technical expertise to resolve individual problems and issues. The latter approach has the advantage that it requires less extensive documentation. The former approach has the advantage that it supports less experienced personnel.

## Considerations

Because no environment is perfect, procedures to address what may go wrong are invaluable. The challenge comes in predicting what may go wrong. The most effective help desk procedures are those that are evolutionary, building on past experience and on the most recent support experiences of others.

## Human Resource Plan

### Purpose

The human resource plan, in its many forms and formats, provides an understanding of when and how team members will be applied to the project and to what degree. A natural extension of the project plan, the human resource plan defines what resources are required to achieve the project goals.

### Application

The human resources plan is used on a variety of levels. For senior management, it identifies all of the resources that have been delegated to a given project and the degree to which they will be working on that effort. For the project manager, it provides pinpoint information on which resources are working on which tasks. For the team members, it affords them the ability to know what they will be working on, for how long, and with whom.

### Content

The human resources plan includes either the names or the skill sets of the resources assigned to the project and the degree to which they will be used. Normally, this information is juxtaposed with the activity list or the work breakdown structure. In either case, it is ideal when the list (and concurrent resource usage) can be condensed into summary levels for management review and then broken out into extensive project detail for team member application. The chart should incorporate the resource, the time and degree of usage, and the task or areas to which the resource is being applied.

### Approaches

The human resources plan can take on a variety of forms, including resource histograms (either team or individual), line charts, or spreadsheets with allocations over time. Each approach has its advantages. The resource histogram, such as that shown in Figure 4.4, provides a simple, one-resource perspective on task loading. If

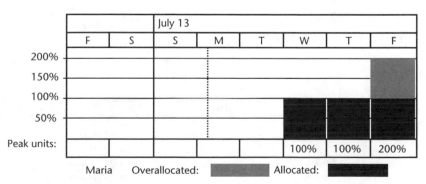

**Figure 4.4**  Resource histogram.

an individual is loaded at a level greater than 100% of its availability, it is highlighted on this chart.

Human resource plans may also be reflected by name, hour, and responsibility in resource spreadsheets, like the one depicted in Figure 4.5. They can also simply be aligned with the work breakdown structure, as shown in Figure 4.6.

Regardless of the choice of the display tool, the human resources plan should reflect when team members will be deployed on tasks and the degree to which they will be applied.

### Considerations

The human resources plan, while seemingly innocuous, can actually become a source for controversy, because it involves individuals and how and when their time will be applied. Also, in some environments, the more detail that is provided on resource utilization, the more upper management will micromanage the effort. For this reason, summary views (rather than task-by-task views) are often desirable when presenting the human resource plan to senior management.

## Integrated Change Control Procedures

### Purpose

Integrated change control procedures are designed to allow for consistent change control from project to project and from activity to activity. The concept is that change control protocols should be sufficiently consistent that they will be able to be employed across multiple projects. Integrated change control procedures will also afford sufficient flexibility to account for customer-specific adaptations as required under contract.

| Resource Name | Work | Details | M | T | W | T | F | S | July 20 S | M |
|---|---|---|---|---|---|---|---|---|---|---|
| ⊟ Bob | 32 hrs | Work | 8h | 8h | 8h | 8h | | | | |
| Task 1 | 16 hrs | Work | 8h | 8h | | | | | | |
| Task 3 | 16 hrs | Work | | | 8h | 8h | | | | |
| ⊟ Maria | 48 hrs | Work | | | 8h | 8h | 16h | | | 16h |
| Task 2 | 16 hrs | Work | | | 8h | 8h | | | | |
| Task 4 | 16 hrs | Work | | | | | 8h | | | 8h |
| Task 5 | 16 hrs | Work | | | | | 8h | | | 8h |

**Figure 4.5**   Resource spreadsheet.

| Task Name | Start | Finish | Resource Names |
|---|---|---|---|
| Task 1 | Jul 14 | Jul 15 | Bob |
| Task 2 | Jul 16 | Jul 17 | Maria |
| Task 3 | Jul 16 | Jul 17 | Bob |
| Task 4 | Jul 18 | Jul 21 | Maria |
| Task 5 | Jul 18 | Jul 21 | Maria |

**Figure 4.6**   Resource table.

### Application

These change control procedures are used in virtually every project, because they provide consistency in how change control is implemented. They are used to provide guidance on how change should be assessed, managed, and documented for all projects in a division or organization.

### Content

The detail of integrated change control procedures looks virtually identical to any change control plan (see earlier section). The only major difference is that integrated change control will have management approval at a higher level (for the process, not the changes) and will address the need to assess the impact to other projects (as well as the project causing the change).

### Approaches

The integrated change control procedures are monitored by the PMO or the PSO. Those groups provide guidance on how to adapt when contractual requirements force modifications in approach or documentation. That guidance normally consists of a review of the process, highlighting which steps in the process have been modified or eliminated. The details are reflected in the individual project change control plan (as appropriate).

### Considerations

Integrated change control is normally the province of more mature and larger project organizations, where consistency is critical to project and program success. Because larger organizations more frequently switch project personnel, there is a greater need for integration of practice. Integrated change control requires monitoring and discipline. As such, organizations with a PMO or PSO are more likely to have the resources to police the process.

## Issue Management Plan

### Purpose

The issue management plan is a clear description of how the organization (or individuals) will contend with environmental, cultural, technical, and project-specific concerns that either exist or will inevitably come to pass. Because issues are conditions that must be dealt with (unlike risks, which may or may not occur), the issues management plan identifies concerns that must be either acknowledged or addressed.

### Application

The issue management plan is primarily used in two environments: management reporting and problem tracking. For management reporting, the plan is used to raise management awareness of concerns (in many cases, concerns that they have authority to help reconcile). For problem tracking, the plan is shared with team members to ensure a consistent understanding of project issues and how they are being addressed.

## Content

The issue management plan includes details on specific issues and their potential resolution. Dealing with specific issues allows managers to avoid those issues that are simply endemic cultural conditions (e.g., the team is spread all over the world), instead focusing on the project-oriented particulars (e.g., with one team in Kuala Lumpur and another in the United States, attendance at virtual meetings is consistently spotty). The difference allows the project manager, team, and management to understand the true nature of the problem and, ideally, to identify solutions. Once an issue is raised, its status is updated regularly either through the end of the project or until it is uniformly considered resolved.

Some issue management plans incorporate ownership designations for each issue to ensure that someone is tracking the issue and determining whether or not escalation to a higher level of management is appropriate.

## Approaches

The key in issue management is to make it separate and distinct from risk management. Some organizations approach this by formatting risk management plans and issue management plans in similar tables, making the only distinction one of the nature of the two (risks may happen, while issues exist). Table 4.3 is an example of an issue management plan.

## Considerations

Many organizations attempt to blur the line between issues and risks. Because risks are future phenomena, they require different types of assessment and management—and because issues are already in existence, they must be dealt with (or at least acknowledged) in real time. If team members, managers, and customers are not made aware of the distinction, there may be the expectation that all risks will be reassessed in real time, or that issues can be prioritized based on when or if they might occur. Those misconceptions can lead to mismanagement of the issues and/or risk events.

**Table 4.3**  Sample Issue Management Plan

| Issue | Area of Impact | Current Degree of Impact | Resolution Strategy | Issue/Strategy Owner | Next Review Date |
|---|---|---|---|---|---|
| Full sentence narrative describing the problem | Specific individual, function, customer, product, or other area of impact | Current condition of the area of impact, based on the issue | How the issue is being handled or managed or will be managed in the future | Team member name responsible for the issue and strategy | Date for reassessment of the issue, impact, and strategy |

## Kickoff Meeting Agenda

### Purpose

The kickoff meeting is one of the most critical elements of the planning phase, because this is the meeting at which team members, project managers, vendors, and the customer gather together for the first time. It is the opportunity to set the stage for the remainder of the relationship. Thus, the kickoff meeting agenda becomes one of the first true planning documents to be shared universally with all project stakeholders. It provides the outline of what will happen at the kickoff meeting.

### Application

A kickoff meeting agenda is used for both the internal and external kickoff meetings to inform participants about the topics to be covered, the schedule, and the general intent of the meeting. It is provided, in advance, to all participants to allow them time to evaluate the meeting approach and to determine if there is any supplemental information they will need to gather prior to the meeting.

These meetings can be used internally to ensure that all participants convey the same messages to the customer. They can be used with external stakeholders to build a sense of excitement about the project and to ensure that the project organization's vision for the effort is aligned with the vision of the customer. Internal and external kickoff meetings are normally different meetings with different objectives. The common elements for both include the effort to build the team and the clarification of project objectives.

### Content

Kickoff meetings must include a general overview of the project and the project organization's approach to delivering the project. But the meeting often affords the first (and in some cases, only) opportunity for all of the project stakeholders to be introduced and to clarify their roles in the project. An outline for a rather exhaustive kickoff meeting may also include a lot of initial planning activities as well.

#### Sample Kickoff Meeting Agenda

**Participants: (Names/Organizations)**

**Date:**

**Time:**

**Place:**

1.0 Welcome and Project Overview

The welcome is often conducted by the project manager, but this task may also fall to a senior-level executive within the organization. Some organizations prefer to have high-level executives introduce the project to give the participants a sense of the relative level of importance of the effort.

The overview provided here should draw directly from the contract, statement of work, or memorandum of understanding that is driving the effort. Although the project organization's approach to the work may be discussed at a high level, this is a general statement of scope and intent.

## 2.0 Introductions: Roles and Responsibilities

The introduction of team members and their roles may afford an opportunity for team-building activities. Team members should identify not only their organizations, but also the nature of the work they will conduct on the project; this may provide an opportunity for team-building activities through shared introductions (having team members talk with and introduce each other) or through other creative introduction approaches.

Regardless of the nature of the introductions, they should be time constrained; otherwise, this activity can potentially affect the remainder of the meeting's schedule if not monitored and controlled well.

## 3.0 Project Intent

This component may be conducted by the customer and/or project sponsor. They present their views on what they believe the project should accomplish and how the effort will be accomplished. This allows the customer and/or sponsor to introduce their vision of the condition of their organization after the project is completed. It can also serve as affirmation of the project organization's approach as the meeting continues.

## 4.0 Intent Q&A

A brief, time-limited question-and-answer session allows the stakeholders to affirm their understanding of the project intent.

## 5.0 Project Approach

This component will be conducted by the project manager or his designee to review how the project organization intends to achieve the project intent. This should be a high-level review of a variety of project components, including schedule, shared commitments (between the project and customer organizations), and communications strategies to ensure the best possible outcome. This is frequently the single longest component of the kickoff meeting.

## 6.0 Approach Q&A

A brief, time-limited question-and-answer session allows the stakeholders to affirm their understanding of the project approach.

## 7.0 Breakout Reviews

In larger projects, it is often necessary to break out the attendees into respective project areas or functional groups to allow for a more detailed analysis of the approach. If this is the case, the project manager should have a direct representative on each of the subteams, with the intent that they will report back on their findings and discussions in that group. Those subteam leaders will serve as the smaller group facilitators, and should have a prepared review of what they will discuss and the scope of their project efforts.

### 8.0 Breakout Q&A

A brief, time-limited question-and-answer session allows the subteam members to affirm their understanding of what was said in the breakout reviews.

### 9.0 Stakeholder Commitments

During the Intent, Approach, and Breakout sessions, significant project commitments are often made, including promises to deliver support, documentation, or resources within a given time frame. As the meeting nears its close, these commitments should be documented and reviewed to ensure a common understanding of what activities are pending and what action items will need to be addressed.

### 10.0 Progress and Next Steps

The project manager or senior executive should close the meeting by reiterating the next steps on the project, including any significant activity in the next week or month. There should also be a recapitulation of the accomplishments made during the meeting to reinforce the value of the group activity.

## Approaches

Depending on the scope of the project, meetings of this nature may last an hour or several days. In any case, the determination on duration should reflect the relative project size and complexity. A 6-week project involving 3,000 team members may, out of necessity, need a 2-day kickoff. A 2-year project with a team of three may only need an hour or two of review to get the project going. In addition, the project team should ensure that the right meeting is being held. Internal kickoff meetings allow for a common understanding of internal operations, communications, and interactions in a free and open environment. External kickoff meetings integrate customer and project organizations, and as such, some of the communications must be couched in terms that are acceptable in both environments. A more cautious approach to sharing information is necessitated by the external kickoff meeting.

## Considerations

An invitation to a kickoff meeting can be seen as a badge of honor by those who are invited, because it indicates their role in the project is sufficient to warrant the invitation. Thus, kickoff meeting invitations may become politically charged, because some representatives will want to be invited simply to affirm their political standing in the organization(s). Clear criteria should be established regarding who should attend the meeting so that the rationale used to create the attendees list is unambiguous.

Also, while internal kickoff meetings allow for the free flow of discussion about internal organizational machinations, the external kickoff meetings should not. In some instances, it will be necessary to coach team members (especially subcontractors) about what is appropriate for discussion in the external kickoff meeting and what is not.

## Milestone List

### Purpose

The milestone list (normally coupled with a milestone chart) is used to provide a series of indicators regarding project progress to date and achievements or goals yet to be reached. It gives management a clear sense of specific levels of accomplishment (or consumption). The milestone list affords team members the same information, but more as a gauge of their own levels of achievement.

### Application

The milestone list is generated after the planning process is sufficiently complete that critical process steps have been identified. It is used in management meetings as a simple checklist to clarify which accomplishments have been met and which have not. Because milestones are binary (either met/complete or not), they present information to management or the customer in a clear, comprehensible form. For team members, milestones provide both a history of accomplishment as well as a set of goals for the future. Every milestone checked brings the project one step closer to fruition.

### Content

There are a wide variety of milestones. Some are rooted in specific levels of work accomplishment, such as a phase or deliverable. As such (and since milestones are binary), they are often expressed in the past tense: "Phase One Complete" or "Prototype Delivered." They may also reflect the passage of time or expenditure of resources. "Project Day 1000" or "Budget 50% Consumed" may be flagged as significant milestones in a major project. The common characteristics are that they reflect a single significant level of accomplishment. The milestone list is the aggregation of the milestones determined to be significant by the project manager, management, the customer, and/or the team. If the customer has a set of distinct milestones that they wish to see, it may mean one project will have multiple milestone lists.

Milestones may be displayed across a timeline in a chart, with an open diamond ($\diamond$) representing a milestone that has not yet been met, and a closed diamond ($\blacklozenge$) representing a milestone that has been achieved. Each of the diamonds (open or closed) should be accompanied by a few-word description of the type of accomplishment the milestone represents.

### Approaches

Some organizations will only track milestones requested by the customer. Others will only track those mandated by the organization's processes. Still others will only select those milestones that motivate the team toward specific goals. The milestone list should reflect project and organizational needs.

### Considerations

Some project managers become overly zealous in their application of milestones, using them to denote even the most insignificant accomplishment. This does provide more detailed tracking, but it also limits the capacity of the milestone to serve as a motivator. The more significant the accomplishment associated with the milestone, the greater its potential to inspire performance.

Some individuals attempt to blur the line between milestones and activities, trying to establish milestones that are "half-complete." That cannot be. Milestones are activities with no duration—they are either complete or not. If a milestone in the milestone list can be identified as "halfway done," it probably belongs in the activity list, rather than in the milestone list.

## Performance Baseline

### Purpose

The performance baseline is also known as the *performance measurement baseline* (PMB). It is the metric benchmark against which project performance in terms of time and cost is measured. Project managers use the PMB to determine cost and schedule variance and to display that information in an S-curve format.

### Application

The PMB is established during the planning phase, once the initial costs and schedules have been developed and approved. The PMB ideally sees little change during the project's life, because it provides insight as to how the project was supposed to perform (versus how it actually evolved and performed). For management, it provides the ability to review the original projected spending for the project over time. For project managers, it provides a tool to later establish a sense of the relative levels of variance. For team members, it affords an objective perspective on their targets for spending over time.

### Content

The PMB may take the form of a graph or spreadsheet analysis of the spending plan (Figure 4.7). It consists of incremental and/or cumulative spending projections mapped against the timeline. It can be depicted through a line graph, bar chart, or both.

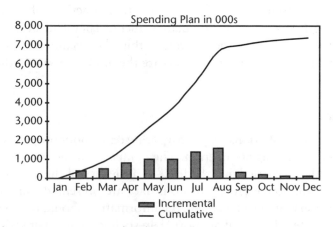

**Figure 4.7** Performance measurement baseline.

The content is normally derived from the project management software package being used to construct and track the work breakdown structure, the costs of the WBS work packages or control accounts, and the timing of those work elements within the network schedule.

### Approaches

The PMB may be used as a stand-alone document for historical reference, or may be coupled with actual spending information later in the project to afford some clarity on the actual spending versus the original plan. It can also be incorporated with earned value information to highlight performance in terms of work accomplished against the original plan for cost and schedule.

### Considerations

Some project managers like to update their PMB regularly to accommodate the myriad changes that are inevitable on a project. While the changes may be authorized and funded, they should not be directly integrated into the baseline, because management requests for baseline information often point back to the original documentation. Questions often surface about why current spending does not match the baseline, and without the original baseline for history, it is difficult to provide meaningful responses to such inquiries.

## Project Customer Presentations

### Purpose

Customer presentations provide opportunities to share the latest insights about a project with the customer. They are often used to sell the project or its progress to the customer and to engender greater levels of customer support for the project delivery organization. They are designed to persuade.

### Application

Presentations are used in the sales environment, as well as the project environment. They can be used to communicate the intent or actions of a project "up" the organization to higher echelons of management. They can be used to provide current project information to peer levels within the organization or to provide training and/or direction to customers who are the ultimate users of the project processes or deliverables.

### Content

Customer presentations may incorporate data about projects which are proposed, in process, or nearing completion. The content and the tone of the content should be respectful, acknowledging the level of authority of the customer and their commitment of time to the presentation. If data are presented using presentation software (e.g., PowerPoint or Freelance), the information should be kept to a reasonable level on each slide. The rule of no more than six lines of text per slide and six words of text per line affords a reasonable guideline. If graphics are presented, they should be legible, clear, and not overburdened with text. For example, if a detailed process diagram is to be included, it should be included as an appendix to the content, rather than presented as a whole in the presentation. Specific elements of the diagram can be called out in the presentation, but most detailed processes are too ornate to effectively fit in a single presentation slide.

## Approaches

The approach should be clear and direct, following an outline that tells the customer precisely the intent of the presentation and delineating how that intent will be achieved. An outline for a customer presentation should identify purpose, means, and detail, as discussed in the following subsections.

### 1.0   Goal/Objective

This should include detail on what the outcome of the presentation will be. In a sales presentation, it would be the ultimate changes to the organization as a result of the project management "buy." In a status presentation, it would be a call for affirmation that the project is headed in the right direction.

### 2.0   Means

*2.1   Delivery Organization Role(s)*   This should delineate how the delivery organization will contribute or achieve the goal or objective.

*2.2   Customer Role(s)*   This should provide details about the role of the customer and her organization's role in contributing to or achieving the objective.

*2.3   Shared Role(s)*   This should outline how the parties will work in concert to achieve the goals or objectives described.

### 3.0   Support

Supporting information will make the case for the objective and the means, providing sufficient background to identify why the customer should concur with the objective and the approach to achieving that objective.

### 4.0   Affirmation

In classic sales parlance, this is where the presenter should "go for the close," reasserting what the project customer is expected to do and how, when, or why they are supposed to do it. It may be as simple as getting an affirmation of support or as complex as setting up a renegotiation of a contract. The affirmation should mirror the objective as stated at the beginning of the presentation.

## Considerations

Presenters may be tempted to incorporate all of the background or supporting documentation for a presentation in the actual presentation software. This can lead to information overload and to presentations that are misconstrued. If large volumes of data are to be presented, they should be broken down into manageable pieces to afford clarity and time for review.

From a visual perspective, the presentation should have a consistent look and feel in terms of the layout, fonts, graphic styles, and language use. Mingling different styles in a single presentation can be distracting.

From a presentation perspective, the presenter should be extremely careful not to simply read the slides verbatim. Although the slides may provide guidance and direction for the project presentation, they should augment the verbal presentation, rather than mirror it.

## Project Plan

### Purpose

The project plan is the guiding document of project management and serves as the repository for all of the subsidiary plans (communications plan, procurement plan, risk plan, and so on). As the guiding document for the project, it inherently needs to reflect all of the information essential to the project manager, project team, customer, and management sponsor.

In summary form, it provides general guidance as to the cost, schedule, and requirements baselines. In its detailed form, it provides much more specific guidance on the nature of all of the components of the various supporting plans.

### Application

The project plan is used by virtually all of the stakeholders in the project. The project manager's primary application for the plan is to settle differences that may arise regarding perspectives in the project. Those differences may exist between team members, the customer and the team, management and the team, or among any of the myriad stakeholders on the project.

For team members and others, the project plan serves as the project "spokesperson" when team members or the project manager are not available to speak on behalf of the project. It gives them insight into the information they are supposed to know and manage during their tenure with the project.

### Content

The summary project plan includes three primary elements made up of the baseline information regarding time, cost, and requirements. Those are normally expressed through a summary work breakdown structure, illustrated in a Gantt chart and accompanied by a spreadsheet of costs broken down by WBS element as shown in Figure 4.8. In a detailed project plan, the level of information is sufficient to provide team members with the baselines for their individual work packages, as shown in Figure 4.9.

The detailed project plan may also include the numerous subsidiary plans that support the project plan:

| WBS | Task name | Duration | Start | Finish | Cost in 000s | Jul 27 S M T W T |
|-----|-----------|----------|-------|--------|--------------|------------------|
| 1 | Project | 23 days | Jul 28 | Aug 27 | $5,816.00 | |
| 1.1 | Summary level | 6 days | Jul 28 | Aug 4 | $1,240.00 | |
| 1.1.1 | Control account | 3 days | Jul 28 | Jul 30 | $424.00 | |
| 1.1.2 | Control account | 4 days | Jul 30 | Aug 4 | $816.00 | |
| 1.2 | Summary level | 8 days | Aug 5 | Aug 14 | $2,208.00 | |
| 1.2.1 | Control account | 4 days | Aug 5 | Aug 8 | $1,200.00 | |
| 1.2.2 | Control account | 6 days | Aug 7 | Aug 14 | $1,008.00 | |
| 1.3 | Summary level | 14 days | Aug 8 | Aug 27 | $2,368.00 | |
| 1.3.1 | Control account | 6 days | Aug 11 | Aug 18 | $848.00 | |
| 1.3.2 | Control account | 14 days | Aug 8 | Aug 27 | $1,520.00 | |
| | | | | | | |

**Figure 4.8**   Project plan.

| WBS | Task name | Duration | Start | Finish | Cost in 000s | Jul 27 S M T W T |
|-----|-----------|----------|-------|--------|--------------|------------------|
| 1 | Project | 23 days | Jul 28 | Aug 27 | $5,816.00 | |
| 1.1 | Summary level | 6 days | Jul 28 | Aug 4 | $1,240.00 | |
| 1.1.1 | Control account | 3 days | Jul 28 | Jul 30 | $424.00 | |
| 1.1.1.1 | Work package | 1 day | Jul 28 | Jul 28 | $96.00 | |
| 1.1.1.2 | Work package | 2 days | Jul 29 | Jul 30 | $224.00 | |
| 1.1.1.3 | Work package | 1 day | Jul 29 | Jul 29 | $104.00 | |
| 1.1.2 | Control account | 4 days | Jul 30 | Aug 4 | $816.00 | |
| 1.1.2.1 | Work package | 2 days | Jul 31 | Aug 1 | $224.00 | |
| 1.1.2.2 | Work package | 4 days | Jul 30 | Aug 4 | $416.00 | |
| 1.1.2.3 | Work package | 1 day | Aug 4 | Aug 4 | $176.00 | |
| 1.2 | Summary level | 8 days | Aug 5 | Aug 14 | $2,208.00 | |

**Figure 4.9**   Detailed project plan.

- Human resource plans;
- Quality plans;
- Risk plans;
- Procurement plans;
- Integration plans;
- Communications plans.

The various supporting plans provide a comprehensive structure that can be used to clarify expectations for the project and its various aspects.

### Approaches

The approaches to project plans are as diverse as the project managers who build them. Because of the varying levels of depth and the various elements that can be incorporated, very few organizations without specific protocols will create similar project plans from one project to the next. The key to sound project plan development is first determining the specific needs the project plan is intended to address. If that can be determined in advance, the appropriate plans can be developed. Many organizations address this issue by establishing clear protocols for project plan development.

### Considerations

The project plan is a living, growing document, evolving as the project progresses. Documentation may be retained in a set of three-ring binders, a set of file folders in a network, or any type of collection or storage media. Wherever it is stored, it should be rendered accessible to team or management members at the appropriate level of depth. All elements of the plan and its supporting plans should not be made universally available. Information should be available on a need-to-know basis, because too much information can be as damaging to project communications as too little.

## Project Schedule

### Purpose

The project schedule provides information regarding the overall project duration as well as each activity's duration. It reflects the project schedule baseline and is used to present that baseline information to team members, management, and the customer.

### Application

The schedule is used to present information on the timing of the project and its activities to a variety of stakeholders (in a variety of ways). It can be used *in toto* or in components.

### Content

The schedule may consist of a project-length timeline, as well as the specific activity information, including the activities':

- Working duration;
- Effort hours;
- Elapsed duration;
- Earliest possible start date;
- Earliest possible finish date;
- Latest possible start date;
- Latest possible finish date;
- Available total float
- Available free float;
- Relationships with other activities.

As a complete set of project activities it can reflect all of the work in the project. As a subset of those activities, or fragnet (a self-contained subset of a project schedule), the project schedule can reflect a time-sensitive window of project activity.

### Approaches

The variety of display options for project schedules are legion. The most common presentation vehicle for project schedules is a Gantt chart, pioneered by Henry Gantt in the early 1900s and illustrated in Figure 4.10. The schedule may also be displayed as a precedence diagram (Figure 4.11), which highlights the network of activities and the relationships among those activities. It can also be depicted as a different type of network, an *activity-on-arrow* (AOA) diagram, as depicted in Figure 4.12. Still other project managers will depict the project schedule with the use of an ordinary calendar (as shown in Figure 4.13).

The choice of tool should largely depend on the application and the level of knowledge and understanding of the stakeholder to whom the schedule is being presented. Some team members may function most effectively through a basic calendar. Management may prefer a Gantt presentation. Those with a process orientation may lean toward the network approaches.

| WBS | Task name | Duration | Start | Finish | Jul 27 S | S | M | T | W | T | F | S |
|-----|-----------|----------|-------|--------|----------|---|---|---|---|---|---|---|
| 1 | Project | 23 days | Jul 28 | Aug 27 | | | | | | | | |
| 1.1 | Summary level | 6 days | Jul 28 | Aug 4 | | | | | | | | |
| 1.1.1 | Control account | 3 days | Jul 28 | Jul 30 | | | | | | | | |
| 1.1.1.1 | Work package | 1 day | Jul 28 | Jul 28 | | | | | | | | |
| 1.1.1.2 | Work package | 2 days | Jul 29 | Jul 30 | | | | | | | | |
| 1.1.1.3 | Work package | 1 day | Jul 29 | Jul 29 | | | | | | | | |
| 1.1.2 | Control account | 4 days | Jul 30 | Aug 4 | | | | | | | | |
| 1.1.2.1 | Work package | 2 days | Jul 31 | Aug 1 | | | | | | | | |
| 1.1.2.2 | Work package | 4 days | Jul 30 | Aug 4 | | | | | | | | |
| 1.1.2.3 | Work package | 1 day | Aug 4 | Aug 4 | | | | | | | | |
| 1.2 | Summary level | 8 days | Aug 5 | Aug 14 | | | | | | | | |

**Figure 4.10**   Gantt chart.

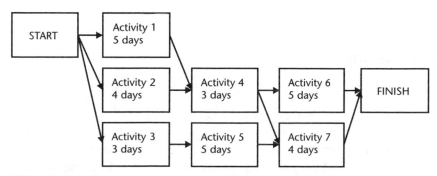

**Figure 4.11**   Network diagram.

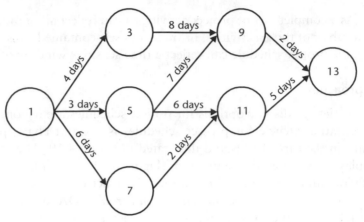

**Figure 4.12**  Activity-on-arrow (AOA) diagram.

| Sunday | Monday | Tuesday | Wednesday | Thursday | Friday | Saturday |
|--------|--------|---------|-----------|----------|--------|----------|
| 27 | 28 | 29 | 30 | 31 | 1 | 2 |
| | Work package, 1 day | Work package, 2 days | | Work package, 2 days | | |
| | | Work package, 1 day | Work package, 4 days | | | |

**Figure 4.13**  Calendar.

### Considerations

If simplicity in presentation is the key, the Gantt and calendar views are normally the preferred approaches. If clarity of relationships is the most important element to understand, one of the network approaches is probably more viable. If the approach is not mapped to the needs of the individual receiving the information, it can be difficult or impossible to detect what is being presented. And because the approaches may include baseline schedule information as well as information about the schedule in process, the sheer volume of data presented can sometimes be overwhelming.

## Quality Management Plan

### Purpose

The quality management plan provides guidance on how quality will be ensured on the project through design reviews, documentation, and other protocols. It gives management and the customer a clear understanding of how quality will be maintained and what documentation they can expect (addressing quality) during the life of the project.

## Application

The plan is generated by the project team and is used as both a cross-reference for other documentation and as a guide for responsibility on the quality aspects of the project. Team members refer to it to find documents (either in whole or be reference) that they need to examine regarding quality standards for their deliverables. Managers refer to it to clarify what practices are considered essential for quality performance and to affirm who is responsible for those practices. The customer may refer to the quality management plan for assurance that quality practices are in place for their deliverables (and to identify any specific practices for which they are responsible).

## Content

Much of the content in quality management plans is often reference. There may be references to performance standard guides, quality standards (like ISO 9000), and internal support documents. The quality management plan is normally limited to a single project or effort within a project and is specific in terms of outlining responsibilities and ownership. The outline of a quality management plan may include the items discussed in the following subsections.

### 1.0 Definition of Scope

This is the scope of the quality plan, not the entire project, expressing how much of the project or deliverables the quality plan is expected to encompass.

### 2.0 Quality Policy

Normally defined in general terms or by referencing other documents, the quality policy expresses the project or support organization's attitude toward quality and quality practices.

### 3.0 Quality Approach

The quality approach often includes extensive reference documentation that supports the quality plan, including the documents needed to validate deliverable performance. It will also outline how specific practices, such as design reviews, management reviews, customer reviews, and records management will be carried out.

### 4.0 Supporting Documentation

For some information incorporated in the quality approach documentation such as flowcharts and external references, copies (or direction to copies) may be embedded as appendices or in supplemental folders.

## Approaches

The depth of the quality management plan hinges largely on the quality practices and policies of the supporting organization. Some organizations with a minimal emphasis on quality may generate an entire quality management plan in a one- or two-page document. Other quality management plans may incorporate binder upon binder of supporting documentation and information.

### Considerations

In developing a quality management plan, it is important to consider the customer's quality practices. Customers with high levels of quality planning and expertise often expect similar levels of effort from their vendors and supporting organizations. Thus, prior to developing a quality management plan, it is often prudent to review the customer's quality practices and management plans.

## Quality Metrics

### Purpose

Quality metrics are the objective measures used to determine whether or not the project and its components are meeting the goals as established early in the project.

### Application

Quality metrics are set early in the project and incorporate some means of measurement that allows for regular interim assessments of progress toward the established objective. Once established, the metrics are used to highlight variance and areas of the project that may require remediation. They can be used to focus on a single area of attention or on multiple areas of concern.

### Content

Quality metrics come in a wide variety of forms and formats, largely dependent on the project type. They consist of an objective measure of the preproject state and a related measure on the same scale of the desired postproject state. An environmental remediation project, for example, might cite the parts per million (ppm) of a given contaminant and the desired postproject ppm count. In a drug research project, a certain level of long-term stability for the output might be measured. For a deliverable within a project, the metrics might include timing, fit, finish, or capacity. Quality metrics can be virtually anything relating to the project or component's desired state that can be effectively measured.

### Approaches

Because quality metrics are measurable, they are most often reflected in bar or line graphs for comparative analysis. They are clear, simple displays as shown with the environmental remediation example in Figure 4.14. The key is to be able to identify, in a metric form, what constitutes project success.

### Considerations

Some quality metrics reports may have dozens of tables, each displaying a different subset of information. Effective use of quality metrics means ensuring that each of the metrics chosen is a meaningful measure to determine the potential success of the project.

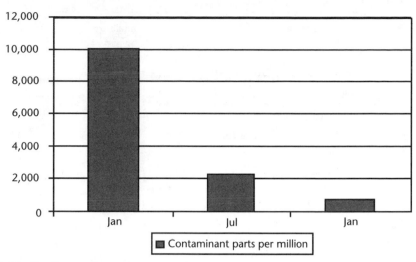

**Figure 4.14** Quality metrics.

## Resources Plan

### Purpose

The resource plan establishes the anticipated use of human and material resources for the project. It defines when and how resources will be applied to allow functional managers to determine how to allocate their personnel and material. It lets team members know when they are expected to participate in the project and the degree of that participation. The resources plan also allows the project manager to review the breadth of resource allocation for the project.

### Application

The resources plan is used to present resource information in terms of their timing, activities, or deliverables. It is often built in the project management software, allowing for ongoing updates and modifications to the allocations.

### Content

The resource plan normally consists of a list of resources and may include their tasks, their costs, and/or their allocation over time. One of the simplest approaches outlines the resources, the work packages to which they are assigned, and the consumption of hours as shown in Figure 4.15. The content may also include hourly rates and the cost by activity or time frame.

### Approaches

The type of information that is incorporated in a resource plan can be presented in a variety of ways, including bar graphs (resource histograms) and spreadsheets. The choice of approach will largely hinge on the information being presented and the emphasis desired. If users desire a quick, at-a-glance consumption rate on the resources, then the bar chart is the most desirable display format. If more detailed

| Resource name | | Work | Details | August 3 | | |
|---|---|---|---|---|---|---|
| | | | | S | T | F |
| Bob | | 48 hrs | Work | 8h | | |
| | Work package | 8 hrs | Work | 8h | | |
| | Work package | 40 hrs | Work | | | |
| Carol | | 32 hrs | Work | | 24h | 8h |
| | Work package | 16 hrs | Work | | 16h | |
| | Work package | 16 hrs | Work | | 8h | 8h |
| Dave | | 56 hrs | Work | | 24h | 8h |
| | Work package | 8 hrs | Work | | 8h | |
| | Work package | 32 hrs | Work | | 16h | 8h |
| | Work package | 16 hrs | Work | | | |
| Edwina | | 72 hrs | Work | | | |
| | Work package | 8 hrs | Work | | | |

**Figure 4.15**   Resource plan.

information (including cost information, specific hours consumed, and other data) is essential, then the spreadsheet would be more appropriate.

### Considerations

Because functional managers are often intensely interested in the activities of their resources (on loan to projects), it is frequently prudent to ask the functional managers what information they would like to see in the resource plan, even though the project manager may be the primary user of the information. Because the information must ultimately be shared with the resource owners (whether the resources are material or human), their desired format for the information may be a critical decision-making factor in selecting the right approach.

## Responsibility Matrix

### Purpose

The responsibility matrix highlights the individuals responsible for certain deliverables or activities within a project. It is used to convey to team members, management, and (in some cases) the customer information about who will be responsible for which deliverables and activities.

### Application

The responsibility matrix is often posted visibly to ensure that all concerned stakeholders can readily determine who has responsibility for particular activities or deliverables. It can provide information on both overall responsibility as well as levels of support or secondary responsibility among other project participants.

### Content

The responsibility matrix normally consists of a matrix of project team members (or stakeholders) juxtaposed against project deliverables, activities or objectives, as shown in Figure 4.16. The content does not normally include extensive information

Responsibility matrix

| | Task 1/<br>Deliverable 1 | Task 2/<br>Deliverable 2 | Task 3/<br>Deliverable 3 | Task 4/<br>Deliverable 4 | Task 5/<br>Deliverable 5 | Task 6/<br>Deliverable 6 | Task 7/<br>Deliverable 7 |
|---|---|---|---|---|---|---|---|
| Ramone | S | | R | | | R | |
| Miguel | | R | | | | | |
| Marianne | | | S | | | S | |
| Juanita | | S | | R | | | R |
| Joao | | | | | S | | S |
| Angel | | | | | R | | |

R = Responsible
S = Secondary

**Figure 4.16**   Responsibility matrix.

about the nature or types of responsibility; it merely identifies the individual(s) who will ultimately be held accountable for project task performance.

### Approaches

As Figure 4.16 illustrates, the types of information provided in the responsibility matrix can vary. For some tasks or deliverables, there may be no need to identify secondary or supporting responsibility (as is the case with Task 4 in Figure 4.16). For others, there may be cause to have multiple individuals in the secondary or supporting role.

The one case that is never appropriate in a responsibility matrix is one in which a task has no one with responsibility (as in Task 1 of Figure 4.16). Ultimately, if a task or deliverable is truly important to the organization and its success, then someone must have responsibility for performance.

### Considerations

The responsibility matrix is among the simplest display tools of project management. There is very little additional instruction or information that need be shared to ensure that its message is clearly understood. As such, managers may be tempted to supplement it with other information or to blend it with other project management tools. The advantage of using the responsibility matrix is that it is so simple. Because of that simplicity, there is very little need to communicate verbally to define the information is provides. It is comprehensive in its coverage.

## Risk Management Plan

### Purpose

The risk management plan lays down the groundwork for how risk management will be carried out in a project. It serves as guidance for the risk process, its thresholds, and its formats, defining the roles and responsibilities of stakeholders in risk management. It is notable that the risk management plan is not a listing of specific risks and is not used to establish the particular strategies for risks, once they are identified.

### Application

The risk management plan is shared with project stakeholders to clarify their roles and responsibilities in the risk management process and to identify when specific potential risks are truly of concern to the organization. It also outlines the risk budgeting process, detailing how and when risk contingency funds may be allocated and applied.

### Content

The risk management plan consists of basic information about how risk management will be conducted during the project. It does not address specific behaviors associated with specific risks, but instead forms a framework for the rest of the risk management process.

### 1.0    Risk Process

Risk process may be as simple as two steps (e.g., assessment and response) or as complex as six or seven steps (e.g., planning, identification, qualification, quantification, response development, and response control [3]). The process steps should include clarification on how each of the processes will be carried out and the level of depth of information to be provided for each.

### 2.0    Risk Responsibilities

Just as the buyer and seller in project environments have different responsibilities for deliverables, so do they have different responsibilities for risks. Those responsibilities should be outlined here. Responsibilities may include information on who will identify risks, as well as who should evaluate them and develop strategies for those that are of the greatest significance.

### 3.0    Risk Thresholds

Thresholds represent personal and organizational tolerance for risk. They are the definitions of tolerance in terms of budget, schedule, requirements, and other sensitive cultural issues (e.g., politics, media exposure). They are normally expressed as ceilings beyond which the project should not proceed, or as notification points for upper echelons of management.

### 4.0    Risk Finances

This element of the risk management plan may address both funds set aside for risks within the project (contingency reserve) and funds set aside within management control for risks outside the project's purview (management reserve). In both cases, this component of the plan details how and when the project team may draw down funds from those reserve accounts. Risk finances may also provide detail on how the amounts for the reserve accounts will be established.

## 5.0 Risk Evaluation

Because evaluation protocols vary from project to project, the risk management plan should include some detail on how risks will be scored and termed. Particularly for risk qualification, there should be some definition of terms for both the probability of a risk's occurrence and for the impact should it come to pass. Many projects employ the *high–medium—low* (H-M-L) scheme for both impact and probability. The risk management plan should define each of those terms.

## 6.0 Process Timing

High-risk projects may require frequent risk reevaluation. Projects with lower risk may not require such frequency. The risk management plan should include detail on the frequency of risk identification, assessment, and response development, as well as the appropriate application of any tracking processes or documentation.

## Approaches

For each of the components of the risk management plan, the approaches may be widely varied. The key is to ensure some measure of consistency from project to project within an organization. One example is provided here:

### 1.0 Risk Process

Risks shall be identified during an initial brainstorming session engaging all available team members. (Risks shall be identified using full sentences to clarify the nature of the negative effect they may have on the project and/or the organization.) They shall be evaluated using the H-M-L scheme defined herein by the project manager and/or his or her designee. Those risks achieving a score of M-H or greater shall be posted on the team watch list, and strategies will be determined for each. Strategies will become tasks embedded in the team activity list and will be assigned to individual team members. They will be tracked as activities in the project management software in a risk table and will be updated to reflect current status. The process shall be updated at least once every 2 months.

### 2.0 Risk Responsibilities

The project manager shall serve as the risk coordinator. Martin L. will serve as the team's risk archivist both in updating the project management software and in providing risk reports to management on an as-needed basis. Team members shall be responsible for their assigned risk activity. John C. will document minutes from all risk meetings and be responsible for disseminating them within 3 days of the meetings' conclusion.

### 3.0 Risk Thresholds

Any individual risks that (if they come to pass) will exceed these thresholds should be escalated to the project manager's attention immediately for further dispensation.

Budget: $20,000;

Schedule: any impact to critical path tasks;

Requirements: any requirement impact that would ultimately be visible to the customer or change the nature of the deliverable;

Politics: any risk that could prompt a client phone call to executive management by a customer or end user.

### 4.0   Risk Finances

Risk contingency for this project is established at 8% of the total project budget. These funds may be allocated by completing Form 517W, identifying the specific nature of and rationale for the allocation. Completed forms should be submitted to Nancy A. in Accounting.

### 5.0   Risk Evaluation

For this project, the following evaluation criteria apply:

Probability

*High*—Happens frequently. Few projects *don't* have this occur.

*Medium*—As likely as not. (Default for uncertain risks.)

*Low*—Could happen. It has been seen on at least one project before.

*Remote*—Very unlikely. Never been seen, but still plausible.

Impact

*High*—Cost: More than $10,000. Schedule: Affects a critical path task. Requirements: Visible to the customer or changes nature of the deliverable.

*Medium*—Cost: $1,000–$10,000. Schedule: Affects any task with less than 3 days of total float. Requirements: Visible internally, no change to the nature of the deliverable.

*Low*—Cost: Less than $1,000. Schedule: Affects tasks with 3 days of total float or more. Requirements: Invisible to all save the original developer.

All medium–high (probability–impact) items will be evaluated for risk strategies and added to the tracking list.

### 6.0   Process Timing

The process shall be conducted at least once every other month.

## Considerations

Because risk management plans are designed to encourage some measure of consistency in risk management practice, they can often be recycled or reused from project to project. If that's done, the key is to ensure that the risk thresholds are appropriate for the current project and that the responsibility assignments are updated to reflect the members of the current project team.

# Risk Mitigation Plan (Risk Response Plan)

### Purpose

The risk mitigation plan (also sometimes referred to as a risk response plan) communicates how specific risks will be dealt with and the action steps that are required to carry them out. It gives team members a clear sense of the actions that they are expected to take and provides management with an understanding of what actions are being taken on their behalf to ameliorate project risk.

### Application

The plan is frequently applied in the project management software as a series of tasks in addition to those that were on the original activity list. The risk mitigation plan may also identify specific triggers, which are events that spur action based on the escalating proximity of a given risk. As risks become imminent, the risk mitigation plan identifies what actions should occur and who is responsible for implementing those actions.

### Content

The risk mitigation plan is a list of specific actions being taken to deal with specific risks. It often lists the names of the individuals responsible for carrying out those actions, as well. Ideally, it is an evolutionary document, capturing information on the outcomes of the risk strategies for future reference.

It can be developed in a tabular format in a spreadsheet or in project management software, using the supplemental text fields that are available in most software packages (Table 4.4). The latter approach is particularly effective when risks are identified and associated with specific work packages within the work breakdown structure.

The plan may include guidance on how to write risk event statements, as well as how to write strategy or response statements. In general, both are significantly enhanced when written as full sentences detailing the nature of the risk and/or strategy under consideration.

### Approaches

In defining risk responses or mitigation strategies, the Project Management Institute acknowledges four basic approaches: avoidance, acceptance, mitigation, and deflection. Whatever approaches are applied, definition of terms will be essential in crafting a sound mitigation plan. The document should incorporate reference to the terms and what they mean:

**Table 4.4**   Tabular Format for Risk Mitigation Plan

| Work Package | Risk Event | Probability | Impact | Strategy | Individual Responsible | Outcome |
|---|---|---|---|---|---|---|
|  |  |  |  |  |  |  |

*Avoidance:* To eliminate the conditions that allow the risk to be present at all, most frequently by dropping the project or the task.

*Acceptance:* To acknowledge the risk's existence, but to take no preemptive action to resolve it, except for the possible development of contingency plans should the risk event come to pass.

*Mitigation:* To minimize the probability of a risk's occurrence or the impact of the risk should it occur.

*Deflection:* To transfer the risk (in whole or part) to another organization, individual, or entity.

The risk mitigation plan or risk response plan should also include some guidance on the frequency of updates to the documentation.

### Considerations

If the risk mitigation or risk response plan is maintained separately from the project plan as a whole, it will be treated as a separate level of effort. Ideally, it should be integrated with other project plan documentation to ensure that it becomes part of the routine associated with project planning.

## Schedule Baseline

### Purpose

The schedule baseline is a real or theoretical construct that captures the approved schedule. It is used to provide a comparison or contrast with the actual progress of work against the schedule and to determine if performance to date is within acceptable parameters.

### Application

The baseline is normally maintained with other project information in either project management or spreadsheet software. It is used both for comparison and reporting, and is normally a critical element in project status reports, progress reports, and forecasts. The schedule baseline serves as affirmation of what the project's schedule looked like when the project was originally approved. According to the Project Management Institute, the schedule baseline incorporates any approved changes.

The schedule baseline is developed by networking individual work elements and determining the path or paths with the longest total duration. That path is then compared against the project due date, or it may serve as the determinant of the project end date.

### Content

The schedule baseline includes work element-by-work element detail depicted across the timeline. It can be reflected in a Gantt chart, network diagram, or a simple milestone chart, highlighting important moments in the approved schedule. Regardless of the display approach, the schedule baseline will include the early start time, early finish time, latest possible start time, latest possible finish time, duration, lag, lead, and relationships for each activity in the project.

### Approaches

Because schedule information comes in a variety of formats and can be displayed in the context of networked relationships or a baseline timeline, the formats for the schedule baseline are legion. While the Gantt chart is among the most common, milestone charts highlighting significant events are also relatively commonplace. For all scheduled activities, the activities driving the schedule baseline should be those that the funding organization recognizes as the agreed-on level of effort for the project.

### Considerations

Baselines are fixed. They do not change with the day-to-day ebb and flow of the project. While changes should be reflected with the baseline, the original baseline should remain intact. The only time a baseline should change is when it is rendered meaningless by the sheer volume of changes (either planned or unplanned). Because the baseline serves as the primary metric for evaluating performance as the project progresses, the stability of the baseline is crucial.

## Schedule Management Plan

### Purpose

The schedule management plan establishes how schedule management will be carried out in the project. It serves as guidance for the scheduling process and formats and defines the roles and responsibilities for stakeholders in those processes. It is not the detailed schedule information, but instead explains how that information will be captured, expressed, and modified (if or when necessary).

### Application

The schedule management plan is used by project managers and the project office to define how management practices will be conducted. In some organizations, it may be a standardized document, applied across multiple projects and modified only slightly to reflect the individual resource and delivery requirements of the project. It is used to prevent project managers from reinventing the process every time they face a new project.

### Content

The schedule management plan includes descriptions of required documents (e.g., network diagrams, Gantt charts, milestone charts), as well as some insight on how those documents may be developed.

### 1.0   Scheduling Process

The scheduling process may include both high-level and detailed descriptions of how the schedule and its components will be generated. The process includes information on when the schedule should be baselined and when certain types of documents (e.g., milestone charts, team calendars) should be updated.

### 2.0   Scheduling Responsibilities

The responsibilities should reflect who will be accountable for schedule updates and for capturing real-time information on project and task performance. This may also include who is in charge of the scheduling tools and who is conducting data entry.

### 3.0   Schedule Parameters

Any noteworthy project schedule limitations (e.g., major milestones, finish date) should be identified here.

### 4.0   Schedule Modification

This element of the schedule management plan ties in with change control, in that it details how and when the schedule may be adjusted. For organizations applying critical chain management, this may also include how buffer time may be consumed and how management should be notified when such buffer is consumed.

## Approaches

Although the approaches to scheduling may vary, some of the elements are consistent. The schedule management plan should highlight the major milestones and who is responsible for reporting on those milestones (and to whom). The plan may go into extensive detail on team processing of schedule information or may simply identify a single team member with "go-to" responsibility for all scheduling issues. Because it is integrated with other baseline issues (including cost, requirements, and risk), the schedule management plan should be coordinated with any management plans that have been developed for those areas.

## Considerations

Organizations may forego schedule management plans in deference to organizational process documentation that covers the same issues. As long as there is an accessible resource for the information on how the schedule is developed, updated, and maintained, the essence of the schedule management plan is addressed.

# Scope Document

## Purpose

The scope document is a general term for any document that refines and defines the requirements aspect of the triple constraint of time, cost, and requirements. In this general sense, it provides an overview of what the project is supposed to accomplish and clarifies how those accomplishments will be achieved. It may also provide the team members, customer, and project manager with insight on what is specifically not in the scope.

## Application

The scope document is used as a tool to minimize disputes over what is and is not included in the project. It is not only used to clarify the project's objectives for project organization and the customer, but also for team members and between management and the project manager. Because visions about how a project may be carried out frequently differ, the scope document serves as the unifying tool for those visions.

### Content

The scope document is an expanded version of the scope statement, with far more extensive information. It normally incorporates much of the same information as the scope statement, with expanded detail on stakeholders, requirements, deliverables, features, long-term use/application, and administrative requirements. The outline for a scope document may include the elements discussed in the following subsections.

### 1.0   Introduction/Background

This would include the history and any environmental definitions required to understand the project in general terms and to understand the remainder of the document.

### 2.0   Rationale/Business Opportunity

As a cross-reference to the business case, this component expresses the advantages of moving ahead with the project and why it was undertaken. The location of the original business case should be included here.

### 3.0   Stakeholders and End Users

This will list both business areas and individuals, citing their responsibilities, involvement, and any responsibilities or deliverables they may generate associated with the project.

### 4.0   Project Detail

This will sometimes be broken out into the functional requirements for the project and the technical requirements. In some instances, the scope statement may only include the functional requirements. It should incorporate all of the mandatory requirements from the contract or memorandum of understanding, and should incorporate detail on the features of the deliverable that will serve those requirements.

### 5.0   Administrative Requirements

Because administrative responsibilities can be almost as onerous as project deliverable responsibilities, they should be clearly defined as components of the project scope. The information should be included on required meetings, reports, and support for the life of the project.

### 6.0   Postproject Considerations

Because the project effort normally makes up only a small component of a total system life cycle, any long-term considerations that will directly affect the project decision-making process should be incorporated in the scope document. This may include many of the assumptions that will be made regarding long-term application.

### Approaches

Although the scope statement is generally confined to a few paragraphs or pages, the scope document may be a far more substantial document. It captures information from a variety of sources and places it in a single repository. As an alternative, it may largely be a document that provides reference to other documentation in other locations (specifically identifying those locations and the information embedded in that documentation).

### Considerations

Because most of the information included in a scope document can be found in other project documentation, some organizations may choose to forego this document. The only advantage to having a separate scope document is that it provides a single storage area for information that may otherwise be housed in far-flung locations.

## Scope Management Plan

### Purpose

The scope management plan establishes how scope management will be carried out in the project. It serves as guidance for scope process and formats and defines the roles and responsibilities for stakeholders in those processes. It is not the detailed requirements information, but instead explains how that information will be captured, expressed, and modified (if or when necessary).

### Application

The scope management plan is used by project managers and the project office to define how management practice will be conducted. In some organizations, it may be a standardized document, applied across multiple projects and modified only slightly to reflect the individual resource and delivery requirements of the project. It is used to prevent project managers from reinventing the process every time they face a new project.

### Content

The scope management plan includes descriptions of required documents (e.g., functional requirements, technical requirements, change control forms), as well as some insight on how those documents may be developed.

### 1.0 Scope Process

Scope process will include definitions on how the scope for the project will be documented. It will address the nature of functional and technical requirements and the areas/individuals responsible for developing those requirements. It will also include detail on how and when the scope may be modified both before and after the project baseline is established. The process includes information on when the scope should be baselined and when certain types of documents (e.g., change control logs, functional and technical requirements documentation) should be updated.

### 2.0 Scope Responsibilities

The responsibilities should reflect who will be accountable for scope definitions (functional and technical), updates, and real-time information capture on project and task performance. This may also include who is in charge of the scope documentation and who is conducting data entry.

### 3.0 Scope Statement

Either by reference or in whole, the scope statement should be incorporated in this document.

### 4.0 Change Control

Again, either by reference or in whole, the change control process should be embedded in the scope management plan.

### Approaches

Although the approaches to scope management may vary, some of the elements are consistent. The scope management plan should express how and where scope will be definitively captured and how and when it may be modified. The plan may go into detail about how the requirements and scope will evolve (through team processes, expert assessment, or otherwise) or may simply identify a single team member with "go-to" responsibility for all scope issues. Because it is integrated with other baseline issues (including cost, schedule, and risk), the scope management plan should be coordinated with any management plans that have been developed for those areas.

### Considerations

Organizations may forego scope management plans in deference to organizational process documentation that covers the same issues. As long as there is an accessible resource for information on how the scope is developed, updated, and maintained, the essence of the scope management plan is addressed.

## Task List

### Purpose

As the name implies, the task list is the list of tasks or discrete work elements that must be performed to generate the project deliverables. The actual work is defined in sufficient detail such that resources may be allocated to specific efforts to produce specific outputs.

## Application

The task list is used by the project manager to allocate specific work and by the team members to understand their individual responsibilities associated with the project. It can be used in support of network diagramming as the foundation elements for such diagrams, and it may also be used to generate a highly detailed element-by-element cost list in support of budgeting or budget tracking. In its simplest form, it may simply be used as a checklist to indicate what work has been completed and what has not.

## Content

The content in the task list is the list of tasks to be performed on the project. The list may be derived from the work package level of the work breakdown structure or (in some organizations) may be the work package (lowest) level of the WBS. Which type of list is chosen is largely a matter of organizational application. Because the task list is strictly a list of the work to be performed, it may be generated in a tabular format with owners, due dates, and/or degrees of completion (Table 4.5).

Because the task list includes tasks to be performed (rather than strictly deliverables), the tasks included therein should be expressed as verb–object (e.g., "Paint walls"). The verb–object format encourages clarity in task descriptions and helps to ensure that they are, indeed, discrete elements of work to be performed.

## Approaches

Different organizations delineate tasks differently. Some see them as the point at which project responsibilities transition to functional organizations. Others see them as clear, simple, discrete work elements to be performed. The definition on the level of detail associated with the task list is critical. Tasks should, ideally, be roughly of the same scope and size. At the very least, they should all be oriented toward a specific level of accomplishment and reporting.

## Considerations

Some task lists are generated in hopes of "dummy-proofing" a project by ensuring that work is detailed in such granularity that no one will miss a step. Often, such efforts focus so much on discrete detail that larger scale deliverables are overlooked. The task list should be defined down to a level where the project manager is truly interested in the outputs and needs to know when those outputs are accomplished. The task "Stir paint" may need to be carried out, but it is not something most painting project managers would care to know if/when it is accomplished.

**Table 4.5**   Tabular Format for a Task List

| Task No. | WBS Identifier | Task | Owner | Due Date | % Complete |
|----------|----------------|------|-------|----------|------------|
|          |                |      |       |          |            |

# Team Charter

### Purpose

The team charter defines a team's purpose, approach, and infrastructure to support them in carrying out the project. It is a team-oriented document that provides guidelines on behavior, administrative functions, and relationships. It allows team members who are otherwise unfamiliar with their peers on the team to be aware of team expectations and their role within the team dynamic.

### Application

The team charter is developed early in the project by the team to be used as guidance for team behavior and administration. Throughout the project, it may be updated by team consensus, but it is normally posted in a highly visible location to ensure that team members can use it as a reference.

### Content

Team charters vary, but they should work toward developing norms and guidelines for team behavior and performance [4]. That's an important consideration. As such, they can include definition on what team norms are for performance, attendance, and conduct. Team charters may include the items discussed in the following subsections.

### 1.0   Team Objective

This is normally tied to the project objective, but may look at that objective from the team's perspectives on quality, delivery schedules, and cost/incentive accomplishments.

### 2.0   Team Norms

This is a list of behaviors that are either expected or unacceptable within the team. It may include expectations on team meeting attendance (e.g., "Team members who must be more than 5 minutes late for a meeting will e-mail their explanation to those who were in attendance") or protocol (e.g., "Information discussed in team meetings will only be shared outside the meeting through documented minutes") or attitude (e.g., "Team members will avoid the use of the word 'can't' during project discussions"). Although these practices may be difficult to enforce, they establish behavioral norms for team members to understand.

### 3.0   Team Administration

Project team members often need to share significant documentation. The charter includes some detail on where that documentation will be stored, in what formats, and how updates and version control will be maintained. This component of a team charter may also define escalation procedures for team and customer issues. It should also define how and when the team charter may be updated.

### Approaches

Because there are a wide variety of teams, team sizes, and organizational protocols, no two team charters will ever be identical. That affords team members a great deal of latitude in determining what information should or should not be incorporated into the charter. The key in evaluating team charter content is to ask the question: "Will this information potentially minimize conflict or confusion later in the project?" If the answer is "yes," then the component of the team charter should be incorporated.

### Considerations

Team charters formalize information that is frequently given as "understood" among team members. As such, some team members (particularly those with years of service in an organization) may balk at the notion that they should document how their relationship with their peers should function. Also, team charters generally have little or no enforcement capability associated with them. The success of the charter frequently hinges on team members' capacity to become their own team police. If they can capably encourage others to follow the guidance of the team charter, it becomes more effective over time. One means of encouraging adherence is through signatures on the team charter. Although there is still no enforcement capability associated with the document, team members who sign are more likely to adhere to the agreement.

## Testing Plan

### Purpose

A testing plan sets up the framework to determine if the project deliverables are performing in ways in which they were expected to perform. It establishes both the objectives and the game plan for evaluating project deliverables in part or in whole. It also identifies the participants in the process, their roles, and the environment in which the tests will be conducted.

### Application

Initially, the testing plan is used to gain the concurrence of a given audience to the testing approach. It is reviewed by the affected parties to determine if the proper elements are being tested and if the approach to testing truly assesses the efficacy of the element in question. It may be used as a defense of a particular test methodology or tool (or suite of tools) and as a means to validate (or invalidate) assumptions about anticipated test and project performance.

### Content

The test plan includes a description of the test objectives, the environment, and the approach and is generally appended with the outcomes of the tests when they are complete.

## 1.0   Test Objectives

This is a description of what the outputs of the test will be and the project objective those outputs are intended to serve. It may include a description of the level of granularity of the outputs, but generally does not include the anticipated outcome of the test.

## 2.0   Test Approach

This is a description of what approach will generate the outputs described in Section 1.0 and (as available) any historic reference as to why that approach is acceptable, valid, and/or appropriate. This may also include a list of any tools to be applied or methodologies to be pursued, as well as any deviations anticipated from standard testing procedures (if they exist).

## 3.0   Environment and Assumptions

Because the test environment will often determine outcomes, a detailed explanation of the project test environment and any assumptions used to establish that environment should be incorporated in the test plan. This may include details on the duration of the testing, geography or physical location, physical environmental considerations, and cultural or organizational assumptions. This will also include any rationale as to why and how the test environment and these assumptions best emulate the real-world application of the project's deliverables (or the test subject's outputs).

## 4.0   Testing Responsibilities

Either by function or name, the parties responsible for various aspects of the testing are identified, including their respective responsibilities.

## 5.0   Anticipated Outcomes

In some organizations, this element is omitted by standard practice. In others, it is common. Anticipated outcomes identify results the testing is expected to produce. Some organizations omit this component over concerns about possibly tainting the outcomes. Others believe it is a crucial element in assessing organizational capability to determine feasible approaches.

## 6.0   Outcomes

Not completed until after the testing, this element of the test plan is built in to ensure that an historic record of the project testing is maintained. In organizations where anticipated outcomes are documented, this information may be presented in a comparative matrix with the anticipated outcomes.

## 7.0   Conclusions

Based on the outcomes, some conclusions about project or deliverable performance can be drawn. Those conclusions should be rooted in the methodology and data and in their relationship to the original test objectives. This often includes a brief summary of the data that led to the conclusion.

### 8.0 References

Because testing is normally based on scientific approaches or historical information, any references used in developing the test plan, approach, or data should be captured for future reference.

### Approaches

The test plan is intended to create an objective environment in which to evaluate project or deliverable performance. As such, it is important to maintain objective criteria throughout. Metrics are an important component of such criteria, and the test plan should work to ensure that the testing methodology adequately tests for the metrics and that the metrics reflect the desired information.

### Considerations

Test plans often create an ideal environment for the project element being tested. As such, any differences between the test environment and the real world should be clearly called out in the test plan. Also, any external considerations (e.g., weather, resource constraints, scalability) that do not fit within the testing model should be identified as specifically not having been tested. The considerations that were not taken into account may be as critical as those that were.

## Work Breakdown Structure

### Purpose

The work breakdown structure is considered by many to be the key tool of project management. It is a decomposition of the project into its component elements and is used to define the project as a whole. The WBS provides clarification of the project deliverables or tasks (depending on organizational approach or practice). At its various levels, it is used as a work definition tool, a reporting tool, or a project summarization tool.

### Application

The applications for the WBS are as varied as the approaches to using it. In some organizations it is used strictly for work definition, which is accomplished by decomposing work elements (deliverables or tasks) into their parts and subparts. Because the WBS is broken down into different levels, its applications at those levels may vary. And because different organizations break down the WBS in different ways (primarily task- or product-oriented categories), those approaches may lead to different applications as well.

The WBS may be applied in requirements definition by defining the deliverables from the macro to the micro level, until the individual components of the deliverable are clearly delineated. It may be applied in work definition by defining the tasks from the macro level (phase or major task area) to the micro level (individual discrete work elements performed by a given individual or function). It can be applied in cost definition as the smallest component elements are priced out and rolled up to create aggregate cost reports. In the task orientation, the individual discrete work elements can provide a critical input to network diagrams.

### Content

The WBS consists of a variety of levels, each defining the project in greater detail. At the top, summary or highest level, it is normally labeled 1.0 or X.0 (where X is a specific project identifying code), and identifies the project in its entirety. The next level, the 1.1 (or X.1) level, breaks down the deliverable into major components or the project effort into its major tasks. Beyond the X.1 level, there can be a virtually infinite number of further decompositions (X.1.1, X.1.1.1, X.1.1.1.1, and so on), as the project is broken out into more and more finite detail. At the lowest level, however, should be a discrete deliverable or level of effort about which the project manager needs to be aware. The WBS should be defined down to the project manager's level of control.

In some organizations, that lowest level will be predetermined by policy or practice. In others, each project manager must discern the appropriate level of depth for his or her project(s). In any instance, the lowest level of the WBS is referred to as a *work package.*

One level above the work package is the control account or cost account level. The control account or cost account is used primarily for reporting to management, accounting, or the customer.

### Approaches

Given the variety of approaches that are possible with a WBS, the key to any successful approach is consistency. If one section of the WBS is broken out by deliverables, then the entire WBS should be deliverables oriented (e.g., if the 1.2.3 section is a subcomponent, then 1.2.4 should not be a task or task area). For a deliverables-oriented WBS, the breakdown may be defined as follows:

    1.0   Project Description (project) (summary)
      1.1   Key Component (summary)
        1.1.1   Subcomponent (control/cost account) (summary)
          1.1.1.1   Subcomponent part (work package)

The lowest level of that WBS would be a discrete part that is a distinct and separate deliverable. It may be noted that in some major projects, the work package of one organization being supported by major vendors may be the project of the vendor organization.

For a task-oriented WBS, the breakdown may be defined as follows:

    1.0   Project Description (project) (summary)
      1.1   Major task area (summary)
        1.1.1   Subgroup of tasks (control/cost account) (summary)
          1.1.1.1   Specific work element (work package)

The approach is largely driven by either organizational practice or project manager preference, although the U.S. military takes a firm position that the WBS should be a deliverables-oriented document [5].

### Considerations

The WBS evokes passion among some of its users, in that they are ardent that it should be either task or product oriented. As such, when beginning work with a new client or establishing a WBS with a support organization, it is prudent to explore their perspectives and applications regarding the WBS. If they are flexible, existing organizational practice can prevail. If, however, a customer prefers or demands a product orientation and the supporting organization has a history of task-oriented WBSs, some conflict in work definition may ensue.

These actual costs normally include a percentage to acknowledge the organization's investment and expense in administering a project. This burden rate may be different for human and material resources, depending upon the organization's accounting practices. Normally, budget costs are broken out by resources and materials so that the burden for each can be easily incorporated and so that management can discern between human resource costs and material resource costs.

## Conclusion

The planning processes are considered by many to be the heart of project management practice. As such, this chapter includes many of the critical components of project management, including schedules, budgets, and the WBS. These tools have a lasting project impact that affects all off the remaining processes (and, ultimately, the project outcome). As with the initiating processes, it is unlikely that any single organization will use all of these tools, but, as with any good management practice, all of the possibilities should be considered.

## References

[1]    *Why Are Blueprints Blue?*, University of Southern Mississippi Department of Polymer Science, 1999.

[2]    Drucker, P. F., *Management: Tasks, Responsibilities, and Practices*, New York: Harper & Row, 1974.

[3]    *Guide to the Project Management Body of Knowledge*, Newton Square, PA: Project Management Institute, 2000.

[4]    Parker, G., *Cross-Functional Teams*, San Francisco, CA: Jossey-Bass, 1994.

[5]    *Department of Defense Handbook—Work Breakdown Structures*, MIL-HDBK-881, U.S. Department of Defense, Pentagon, Washington, D.C., January 2, 1998.

## CHAPTER 5

# Communications Tools in the Executing Processes

Planning is the core of project management, only because it enables execution. In executing or implementing projects, organizations have the opportunity to make modest changes to the original plans. More importantly, they have the opportunity to capture insight and information as it is developing. The communications tools of implementation are those that capture or share information, reflecting the realities of day-to-day project life. As stated earlier, many (if not most) of the tools deployed here are actually created much earlier in the project processes or may be standard forms or formats used by the organization. They are included in this process because this is where they are executed.

## Acceptance Test Plan Results

### Purpose

The acceptance test results outline which tests were run on a project and the outcomes of those tests. They are used to generate a history of the testing process, as well as the environment and the outcomes.

### Application

The acceptance test results are used to determine whether or not the project deliverables are performing as originally anticipated. If they are, the test results are used as evidence that the customer should accept the project and sign off on any lingering contract documentation. The results also allow for the examination of any anomalies that may occur as implementation moves toward transition to customer-supported operations. If the test results indicate the project is not performing as anticipated, the acceptance tests serve to identify which areas of project performance are not acceptable and what remediation may be required before the customer accepts the project deliverables.

### Content

The acceptance test results will include information about the nature of the project, the tests, the environment, the outcomes, and any reference documentation needed to support the testing methodology. The results may include the information discussed in the following subsections.

### 1.0   Project

This is simply an iteration of the scope statement or a description of the element undergoing testing.

### 2.0   Scope

This is a description of the breadth of the testing, and the nature of the testing (destructive/nondestructive) and the quantity or nature of the deliverables undergoing the tests.

### 3.0   Testing Approaches

This is a detailed description of the types of tests that have been conducted as elements of the acceptance tests and a detailed explanation of how the tests were actually conducted. Specific test cases are identified and the methodology is explained in detail. The test environment is also described here in detail.

### 4.0   Test Results

For the tests identified in Section 3.0, the outcomes of each test are defined. For those that fail or only partially pass, details are provided on the nature of the remediation required or the rationale for the failure. This section may be broken out into general test outcomes and individual supporting component test outcomes.

### 5.0   Current Status

Based on the tests and their results, further action may be required, or the customer may have agreed to some concessions on project performance or approach. Those modifications or additional actions are documented here.

### 6.0   Supporting Documentation

Because many tests, methodologies, and environments are unique, there may be a need for extensive reference documentation to describe the environment. It may be included either in whole or by reference in the acceptance test results.

### Approaches

The level of detail in the acceptance test result documentation should be determined as the project contract documentation is being developed. The level of detail will largely determine the level of effort associated with the documentation. Also, because the outcomes from the acceptance test results often determine whether or not a project is "accepted" and paid for, it is important to have a mutually understood protocol (between buyer and seller) for what will happen after the test results have been generated.

### Considerations

Some customers may deem it essential that every element of a project's test criteria pass before they will accept deliverables. Others will accept some marginal level of failure, as long as it does not exceed a given threshold. That's why it is important to determine how perfect the test outcomes must be before the tests are conducted. It is also important to determine where specific attributes (yes/no, pass/fail) must be met and where other elements will be evaluated on a more variable or gradient scale. The more that can be done to establish expectations early in the project, the more likely the project acceptance test results will be viewed favorably when they are completed.

## Action Item Register

### Purpose

Every project has small, seemingly inconsequential tasks that are the fuel of day-to-day operations. There are phone calls to be made, team members to be nurtured, vendors to be checked on. As such, myriad action items, too small to be labeled as "tasks" or "work packages," must be documented and tracked. The action item register is a log for cataloging and tracking these items and for ensuring that they are addressed in a timely fashion. In some instances, the action item register is generated during status meetings and becomes an attachment to the status report (Chapter 6).

### Application

The action item register is used as a team-oriented document, posted in a common team location (virtual or physical). It is used to affirm that team members know their role in these smaller tasks and understand their responsibilities and the timing for those responsibilities.

### Content

The action item register consists of a list of specific minor tasks to be performed, normally presented in a columnar format. Other columns adjacent to the action items may include the individual responsible, the time the action item was developed, and the anticipated resolution date. There may also be a "Notes" field to document any challenges or concerns that arise associated with the action item or its dispensation. The action item register might look like Table 5.1.

**Table 5.1**    Sample Action Item Register

| Date Added to List | Action Item to Be Performed | Responsible Team Member | Date Due | Date Resolved | Notes |
|---|---|---|---|---|---|
| This may be the primary means for sorting the list, as action item lists evolve over time. | This is a detailed description of the action to be taken and the desired outcome. | Although several individuals may work on the task, a single point of responsibility should be identified. | This should be the date by which the action item should be performed, or a date on which the status of the action item is reviewed. | This is the date on which the action item was closed out, either through performance or because it was no longer needed. | This includes any notes on performance, concerns, or lessons learned for future action items. |

### Approaches

The action item register may be developed in a variety of tools, including simple document tables, spreadsheets, or databases. The information should be stored electronically, so that it can be manipulated to sort by initiation date, responsible part, resolution date, or due date. The information should be presented publicly and updated regularly, to ensure that there is a sense of currency and immediacy to the information.

### Considerations

Action item lists are normally separate and distinct from the work breakdown structure and the task or deliverable information included therein. That's because the WBS covers information at a higher level. The action item list is designed to ensure that lesser tasks that are not directly associated with the deliverables are still resolved. It may be appropriate to place some limitations on the size of action items, because the action item list can become a "back door" means to build in some scope creep into the project.

## Change Control Form

### Purpose

The scope change control form is designed to capture the nature of a change request in a formal document and to serve as a historical, contractual record of the change request and its ultimate dispensation.

### Application

The change control form is filled out whenever a change request is submitted or when a change occurs on the project that will alter the original approach or how that approach will be implemented. It is often completed by designated project team members to ensure that it is completed in a consistent fashion and is processed by the appropriate designees within the organization. It is used to initiate and track changes to the project's scope and to capture project team and customer signatures for the contract record.

A scope change control form documents the nature of the request, the processing required, the current status of the request, the team members notified, and the impact of the change on the project as a whole.

### Content

The scope change control form (Table 5.2) is a repository for information both from the project change request, which may have been either verbal or written, and from the project and customer organizations, in terms of approvals and assessments. Signature fields may include both project team signatures and customer signatures.

### Approaches

Because different organizations have different perspectives on how the customer should be served, the scope change control form may have varied levels of detail.

**Table 5.2**   Sample Scope Change Control Form

| Change Control—Project Change | | | |
|---|---|---|---|
| Requester Name: | Name/e-mail of individual requesting change | | |
| Request Date: | | | |
| Change Description | | | |
| Reason for Change: | Clearly define the business reasons for implementing the change, including names/e-mails of any critical players | | |
| Change Impact: | Specific savings/revenues to be realized as a result of the change or behavioral improvements promoted by the change | | |
| Need by Date: | | Approved for Analysis: | |
| Functional Impact of Change: | Functional Area Affected: Name of Functional Organization<br>Functional Area Affected: Name of Functional Organization | | |
| Schedule Impact: | # Days: | Cost Impact: | $ |
| Approved by: | Name/e-mail of approving authority | | |
| Signature: | | | |
| Denied by: | Name/e-mail of responsible authority | | |
| Signature: | | | |
| Deferred by: | Name/e-mail of responsible authority | | |
| Deferral Review Date: | | | |
| Signature: | | | |

The impact fields are perhaps the most crucial in that they provide the history of the change and insight into the nature of and rationale for the change. Scope change control forms are often the next step in the change process after an initial change request is submitted. And because some of the information collected here is redundant with the information generated in other types of change forms, computerized links to those other forms are appropriate, if the information is generated virtually.

### Considerations

Although e-mail "signatures" are acceptable in some organizations, the physical signature tends to carry more clout on these forms. If e-mail signatures are to be accepted, there should be a specific protocol for what constitutes an "authorized" e-mail versus a standard e-mail for the sake of approvals and responsibilities.

## Change Control Record

### Purpose

A change control record is crafted early in the project by the project manager or procurement office for the buyer in the project, to acknowledge significant change to major components or elements of project work. It allows for the tracking of changes during the early stages of a project, prior to final vendor selection.

### Application

In some procurement efforts, multiple amendments to the original solicitation lead to a need to track those amendments in a single document, supplemental to the original solicitation. The change control record is used by internal buyer personnel as a reference to track what they have changed and how they have changed it. It may also be forwarded to selling organizations to aid in their responses.

### Content

The change control record includes a cover page that lists the various revisions, the date(s) on which they occurred, the nature of the revisions, and the authority (individual) who approved them. The cover page is then supported by detailed scope documentation and supporting information on the nature, rationale, and purpose of the change and any related affected clauses or terms within the solicitation.

### Approaches

The change control record, ideally, will only have a handful of revisions addressed. In some instances, however, the documentation may include more than a dozen modifications to the solicitation. In these more substantial documents, the supporting scope documentation should be developed in a consistent fashion for ease of reference.

### Considerations

Although the change control record may be the purview of the procurement organization, the project manager should refer to the document regularly during the solicitation phase of a contract relationship. This will encourage a shared understanding between the project manager and the procurement office on how and why changes are being implemented.

## Change Requests and the Change Request Log

### Purpose

Change requests are written or verbal statements of need or desire. They reflect a stakeholder's interest in making a modification to the project as proposed, planned, or in execution. The change request log provides a documented record of change requests, as well as their disposition.

## Application

Change requests are used when any stakeholder believes the project or customer organization may be better served by a different strategy or approach to the process or deliverables. Change requests may be initiated by virtually anyone at any level of either the buyer or seller organization. In some organizations, only written change requests will be acknowledged or evaluated, whereas in others, verbal change requests will also be given consideration. The change request log is used as a history of change requests and as a means of tracking their disposition on an ongoing basis.

## Content

The change request, either verbal or written, should include a description of the nature of the change, the source of the request, and the rationale for the request. The change control log catalogs that information, as well as impact information, in a column format, similar to that shown in Table 5.3.

The table may also include cross-reference information, linking the change request to certain contract line items or to elements of the work breakdown structure. It may also include a glossary of terms for "current disposition" and "impact assessment," because different organizations may require different levels of review and approval for changes.

## Approaches

The change request log builds in a measure of consistency into the change management process. It encourages common inputs into the process and a common evaluation approach for all change requests. As a key component of project requirements, the log should be readily available to project team members responsible for project delivery. It should be maintained in a file with read-only access to those who are not responsible for approving or disapproving project change requests. If multiple iterations of the document are being retained over time, a rigid version control process (using dates or 1.X.X codes) should be established to reflect the currency of the document.

## Considerations

Verbal change requests are not uncommon so, ultimately, before their impact is assessed and approval granted, they need to be documented. Many organizations will not accept any change request that is not in writing. Others wait until the change reaches the approval stage before they commit it to paper. In either case, it is essential to capture the history of changes as part of the project document record in order to ensure the right project requirements are ultimately being met.

**Table 5.3** Tabular Format for Change Control Log

| Date | Nature of Change Requested | Rationale and Source | Person Making the Request | Impact Assessment | Current Disposition |
|------|----------------------------|----------------------|---------------------------|-------------------|---------------------|
|      |                            |                      |                           |                   |                     |

# Data Dictionaries

## Purpose

In software projects, the data dictionaries are tools used to track the names, titles, and codes associated with any data elements that will be referenced by the software application. The data dictionary clarifies what the data element should (and should not) include, its type, and its home in the database or storage repository.

## Application

Data dictionaries are used to facilitate software development by clarifying the nature of information being stored and the information types or classes. The data dictionaries allow for inclusion of new data elements without creating an entirely new data element numbering sequence. They also provide developers with the ability to look at the varied types of information available to them in a single document.

## Content

Data dictionaries are simple tables that catalog the data element name, its reference number, its location, its information type, and a description of the information. It may also include the parameters of the data. A sample data dictionary is shown in Table 5.4.

## Approaches

Although the sequence of the headings in data dictionaries may vary, the information is largely similar. Different organizations may add or delete a column or two, but the lion's share of the information is consistent.

## Considerations

Because some software applications and databases draw on dozens of different data elements, the data dictionary may be quite extensive. There may be a temptation to resequence or renumber the data elements whenever a new data element is added to keep the elements both sequential and in alphabetical order. That would be a mistake. Because different software applications often call on the same data elements, the numbering must be consistent within the database, and should not be changed, but merely augmented as new data elements are added.

**Table 5.4**  Sample Data Dictionary

| Data Element Number | Data Element Name | Location | Information Type | Description | Parameters |
|---|---|---|---|---|---|
| This is a numeric code used for consistent calls in software application development. | This is a label used to briefly describe the type of information included in the data element. | This is the physical or virtual place where the data element is stored. | This is the form or format of the information (date, numeric, text, and so on). | This is a more expanded description of the data element. | This establishes the size limits of the data element. |

## Effort Statement

### Purpose

Effort statements may be required by regulation. They are used to certify how employees have invested their time on a project. They identify not only the employee's classification(s), but also the specific tasks he or she worked on and the amount of time invested in those tasks. The depth of reporting will be determined by contract or regulation. In some organizations, effort statements are used to augment the monthly status report with detail on resource allocation and activity.

### Application

The effort statements are external documents, used when the client demands certification of performance.

### Content

They contain a limited amount of information, consisting of the resource name(s) or type(s), the task(s) on which employees worked, and the amount of time consumed while working on the task(s).

### Approaches

The information can be presented in a spreadsheet, table, or list. If the documents are required by regulation, the regulation may specify the formats used.

### Considerations

Effort statements are certifying documents. As such, the expectation is that the information contained therein is going to be accurate. The level of reporting in the effort statement should reflect the level of team member reporting within the time management system used by the organization. If a higher level of detail is required by contract, then before the project begins, tracking mechanisms should be put in place to serve that specific level of reporting to ensure accuracy.

## E-Mail/E-Mail Protocol

### Purpose

E-mails are generally informal internal documents for sharing information. They create a document record and provide a history of information transactions, but do so without the formality of a memorandum (see later section). Although *considered* informal, e-mail transactions can carry formal weight in legal proceedings and are considered part of the organization's historical record.

### Application

E-mails can be used in virtually any setting and for almost any type of information sharing or transfer. They are used whenever there is a need to share information quickly, thoroughly, and asynchronously. They are used when the record may be important to success of the communications loop, but is not necessarily of historical significance.

## Content

Although the information content of e-mail is widely varied, much of the information included in the document headers is consistent. Header information includes a date, the name and e-mail of the sending party, the name(s) and e-mail(s) of the recipient(s), and the subject matter included. The informational content within the e-mail may be short or long form. It may be of a formal or informal nature, but should always be treated as if it might be maintained as part of the permanent record.

## Approaches

In crafting e-mail, there are a number of potential approaches. Project managers in some organizations will dictate the "Subject" information format to include only specific data elements, such as work package number, project name/code, and/or nature of the e-mail (e.g., approval request, informational, customer data, form attached). By generating specific rules for what information may be included in the subject heading, e-mail sorting and filtering can be done more quickly.

### Sample E-Mail Protocol

For all project e-mail, the subject line shall read as follows:

(Work Package Number)—(Name)—(Nature)

- Work package numbers may be derived from the WBS, stored on the LAN at w:/project/projectfile.mpp.
- Name shall be the name of the work package involved (e.g., Foundation Excavation)
- Nature shall be one of the three following categories:
    Approval request
    Informational
    Data (attached)

If an e-mail is not directly related to a specific work package, the header shall read as follows:

(Project Name)—Project Support—(Nature)

No e-mail shall include a "trail" of more than four past e-mail transactions without a summary of those transactions in the first paragraph of the e-mail.

As for the content of the e-mail itself, some basic protocols should be followed. Use of all capital letters for any word or series of words is generally perceived as shouting. Such usage should be minimized. Also, the word *you* is frequently seen as accusatory in e-mail transactions. Although it cannot be eliminated, its use should be very carefully considered. And because e-mails are transacted quickly and can be broadcast to a significant number of project parties, the recipient's list should be limited to those directly impacted by the e-mail's information.

### Considerations

The immediacy of e-mail is both bane and blessing. It is helpful in the project environment because of the frequent need for immediate information transfer. It can be deleterious because it sometimes encourages a "heated" response without time to consider the long-term implications of such a response. Few e-mails are so critical that a 5-minute cooling-off period cannot be applied. In environments where sensitivities are high or where e-mail has generated concerns in the past, such a waiting period may be well advised.

## Gantt Chart

### Purpose

The Gantt chart is the single most popular information presentation tool for project management. It gives an at-a-glance perspective on the names and timing of tasks, as well as their current status. It is used to highlight a project's triple constraint of time, cost, and requirements and affords an at-a-glance perspective on project variance.

### Application

Gantt charts are used to present information to management, team members, and customers at a variety of different levels. Some Gantt charts are used at a summary level to provide a one-page or few-page perspective on project activity. Some are used with work package-by-work package information to allow team members to see the range of tasks being performed and the status and timing of those tasks.

### Content

A Gantt chart consists of a list of project activities, coordinated with a horizontal bar chart to reflect activity duration (Figure 5.1). Note that the first three work packages have bars that differ from the others. The Gantt may reflect levels of completion using such notations. It can also use "split bars" to highlight the original project baseline and to contrast that information with the actual timing of the project as performed.

### Approaches

Gantt charts can be presented in a variety of ways. The simple bar chart is most common in modern project management software packages. Most also have the option, however, of presenting the timing bars with distinct beginning and end nodes as shown in Figure 5.2. The open triangles represent the original plan; the closed triangles provide information on when the tasks actually began and finished.

### Considerations

Software that will produce Gantt charts also generates spreadsheet information. With dozens of fields available, it is possible to display the Gantt chart along with

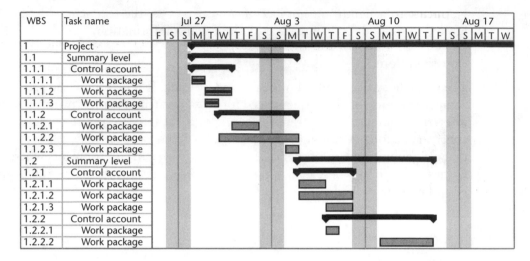

**Figure 5.1** Gantt chart.

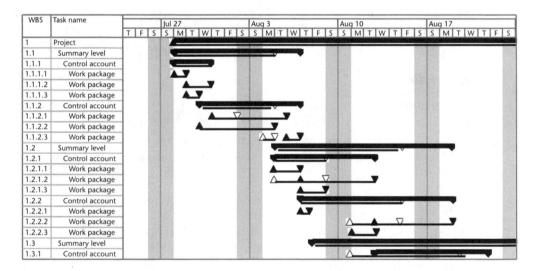

**Figure 5.2** Alternate style Gantt chart. Open triangles = original plan; closed triangles = actual.

information about resources, timing, task status, predecessors, and a host of other information types. Keep in mind, though, that the Gantt chart should not be overloaded with too much information. Only the information germane to the presentation should be included.

# Memoranda

## Purpose

Memoranda are formal internal documents for sharing information. They create a document record and provide a history of information transactions.

### Application

Memos can be used in virtually any setting and for almost any type of information sharing or transfer. They are used whenever there is a need to record the information being presented and affirm that it is a part of the permanent project record.

### Content

Although the information content of memos varies widely, much of the information included in the document headers is consistent. The header includes a date, the name of the sending party, the name(s) of the recipient(s), and the subject matter included. The informational content within the memo may be short or long form.

### Approaches

One of the keys to organizational effectiveness in memo authorship is to ensure that it is sufficiently succinct to allow the reader to absorb the information. A memo should also be written with the expectation that it will become part of the permanent project record. As such, memoranda are not used with the frequency of e-mail. They are also effective in situations where there is a need to prove that communications occurred between two project parties.

### Considerations

Memos sometimes encourage pontification. Since e-mail communication has replaced the memo's traditional position of sharing day-to-day project data, some project team members may use memoranda to share more information, more verbosely. As part of the project record, clarity should be a primary objective.

## Planning Meeting Agenda

### Purpose

Project planning meetings are held, as the name implies, in order to develop all or part of the project plan. They are intended as both data-gathering and data-organization sessions. They are intended to generate not only the project plan, but a consensus on that plan and its implementation. The agenda serves as a guide for how these sessions will be held.

### Application

Project planning meetings may be held any time there is a major shift in project direction or when a new plan needs to be developed. They should be used when a unified vision on how to approach the project is critical (in contrast to situations where a single individual's vision or approach will drive the entire effort). They may be used to generate a single component of the plan (such as the risk plan or schedule) or the entire plan. The agenda should be sent out (via e-mail or in hard copy) to attendees prior to the meeting to ensure that they are aware of the objective, schedule, and approach to the meeting.

### Content

As with a project, the objective of the project planning meeting should be clearly defined. It is important to delineate the specific deliverables and artifacts that will be generated by the end of the meeting, in order to focus effort toward those artifacts. The agenda for a project planning meeting may include a participant list and information about whether they are on-site or "present" via a teleconference. If there are teleconferencing participants, they should be identified as such, because their participation levels will inherently differ from those who are physically present for such a gathering.

### 1.0   Objective

The planning meeting agenda starts with a clear, unambiguous statement of the deliverables or artifacts to be generated by the meeting and the intended use of those deliverables.

### 2.0   Historical Review

Background information is given on the project or subproject to provide a frame of reference as to how and why this set of artifacts is important or significant and why particular approaches are appropriate.

### 3.0   Facilitation of Artifacts

A variety of strategies (addressed below in the *Approaches* section) are used to develop the project plan or components associated with the meeting.

### 4.0   Review and Acceptance of Deliverables

This section contains the participants' assessments of the meeting deliverables.

### 5.0   Review and Acceptance of Action Items

This is where the identification of outstanding action items and assignments is documented.

### 6.0   Adjournment

This is a line item indicating when the meeting is over.

An agenda may be elaborate or simple, but it should include at least the components listed above. The most significant level of effort will be associated with the facilitation of artifacts, because many components of the project plan may be generated for the first time in this meeting.

### Approaches

The approach to the meeting may, in large part, determine the approach to the agenda. The approaches to developing project plans in a group setting are legion. Some project managers will begin with a suggested plan, encouraging participants to add or subtract elements from the plan as appropriate. Others will identify specific elements of the plan to be developed and will work from scratch to build these components. The latter approach requires more significant team coordination and a higher level of facilitation skills.

The facilitation should involve a reiteration of the deliverable and the identification of those individuals present in the meeting who can directly contribute (i.e., those who will actually lead the work or perform the work). Those individuals should be given the first opportunity to provide insight into the approach to the project that would be the most appropriate. The project manager/facilitator may extract this information verbally (through a brainstorming session) or in documentation (either on paper or Post-It notes) for further review by those present. The key role of the facilitator is to ensure that the entire project is covered by the plan and that the project is covered to a consistent level of depth. It is sometimes tempting to cover familiar areas of the project in far greater depth than those areas that are uncharted.

In the effort to build certain components of the plan, conflict is not uncommon. In schedule development using Post-It notes to generate the network, for example, team members may assert themselves aggressively to defend a particular approach or strategy. The facilitator is responsible for stemming such conflicts by working through the issues under consideration toward consensus. For the agenda, be certain to allot more time for facilitation efforts than for simple presentations or discussions.

## Considerations

The agenda sets the tone for the meeting. It should be realistic in terms of the intent and the expectations for the amount of time each agenda item will take. Because project management is largely perceived as a scheduling function or practice, the agenda can often send the message as to whether or not the project manager is capable of adhering to a schedule.

In the meeting, the project manager's role as agenda watcher may be compromised. The project manager may take on a variety of roles in this setting. The project manager may be called on to serve as facilitator, minute-taker, and participant. Regardless of the project manager's effectiveness, no one can serve in all of those roles without diminishing at least one of them. That's why the project managers may want to hire professionals to serve in the roles they do not see as being part of their strengths. Professional facilitators or archivists can keep the meeting moving forward, allowing the project manager to focus on the project and the concerns it raises.

Also, if the meeting includes an extensive body of remote participants, certain types of activities (such as network scheduling) may prove impossible without the use of virtual whiteboards or other Internet-supported interactive displays. If the project planning meeting will include development of any extensive graphic artifacts, the participation modes to be used by remote participants should be considered before the meeting begins to ensure that the setup of these elements does not detract from the agenda.

# Presentations

## Purpose

There are a host of different types of project presentations, but most have the common goal of attempting to sway stakeholders to a particular point of view. As such, they should be aimed at achieving a specific objective, rather than multiple objectives.

### Application

Presentations have diverse uses but are best applied in situations where a single, primary objective is the focus of attention. They should be used in settings where there is a wish to convey a sense of formality as well, because presentations ultimately become part of the permanent project record.

### Content

Presentations should have an introduction that clearly defines the presentation objective and the role of the stakeholders in serving that objective. Beyond that, the supporting evidence for the presentation objective can be defined and a case can be made for stakeholder endorsement of the presentation's case. As an example, a presentation calling for supplemental resources should open with a clear explanation that additional resources are required for certain reasons. The heart of the presentation then continues with the explanation of those reasons and the rationale as to why only those specific resources will suffice to support them. If a presentation is purely informational, then the objective is to ensure that certain individuals can act on certain new data elements.

### Approaches

While computer-generated (PowerPoint, FreeLance) presentations have become the most popular format for presentations, some project managers may prefer to make their presentations without slide support and without formal documentation. For computer-based presentations, the best approaches employ simplicity as a rule. Slide information should be clear and succinct. There should be no more than six lines of text on any given page. No line of text should include more than six words. The simple 6-by-6 rule encourages simplicity and clarity. Information that requires greater depth of understanding should be packaged in handouts or informational supplements.

If graphics and clip art are being used as part of the presentation, they should support a story, point, or informational element either presented previously or on the same slide. Graphics and clip art should be similar in style or format throughout the presentation to enforce a sense of continuity.

The objective should be stated clearly at the beginning of the presentation and again at the end, affirming the stakeholders' role in serving the objective. Presentations tend to be most effective when they engage the participating stakeholders and affirm a level of commitment or ownership to the objective.

### Considerations

Perhaps the most significant considerations in building a presentation are tone and timing. Some presenters can present serious topics with humor and get their point across effectively. Others cannot. The key is to know how (or if) you present well and the best style for your presentations. As for timing, the key in virtually all successful presentations is to make a commitment to a time frame for the presentation and honor that commitment.

## Problem Resolution

### Purpose

The purpose of problem resolution forms, tables, or templates is to catalog problems that have been identified and track the actions taken to resolve them (and the efficacy of those solutions).

### Application

The problem resolution form is used by organizations that have a set of known concerns and a structure for dealing with them. It is not the same as a risk template or a risk mitigation form, in that problems are negative events that have already come to pass, whereas risks are future phenomena that have not yet occurred. The problem resolution form is particularly effective when specific criteria can be established to determine what conditions constitute "resolved."

### Content

Problem resolution includes a definition of the nature of the problem, and the specific requirement, need, or customer concern that is not being met as a result of the problem. It then includes reporting cells for the criteria being used to determine resolution level and the level of performance that constitutes "resolved" or acceptable performance. Date fields for targeted and achieved compliance are also included. Table 5.5 provides a sample problem resolution form.

### Approaches

Problem resolution may be maintained in a table, spreadsheet, form, or any presentation structure that supports the clear and simple sorting of information. Successful problem resolution will involve consistent formats across the organization, so knowledge transfer can be effectively achieved.

**Table 5.5**  Sample Problem Resolution Form

| Problem | Performance Level Unmet | Criteria | Acceptable Performance Level | Targeted Compliance Date | Actual Compliance Date (or Date Dropped) |
|---|---|---|---|---|---|
| This is the issue that exists within the organization. | This is the need, concern, or requirement that is being affected by the issue. | This is the metric being used to determine compliance with the performance level. | This is the specific threshold that should be met (possibly captured as a minimum and maximum level). | This is the date when the acceptable performance level is expected to be achieved. | This is the date when the acceptable performance level was achieved (or the problem was determined to be irresolvable). |

### Considerations

Problem resolution is often confused with risk response because of the similar natures of risk and problems. The two remain distinct and different practices. Problem resolution focuses on specific clear problems to be resolved and the conditions under which they will be resolved. Risk remains far more speculative.

## Prototype

### Purpose

The word *prototype* comes from the Greek for "first impression," which is an apt description of the purpose of a prototype. It is a model created for the first impression of how a final deliverable may look, feel, or function. A prototype affords a first look at a system or deliverable, so that it can be evaluated to determine if full-scale production or implementation is warranted. It can either be a first step in the implementation of a project, or in some organizations, it may be generated as a means to determine if the project approach will be deemed viable and appropriate.

### Application

Although prototypes are most commonly associated with hardware and software implementations, they are actually used in virtually every industry. From galley proofs in publishing to concept cars in the auto industry, prototypes provide the project and customer organizations with an opportunity to examine some of the key features of the final deliverable without the expense and energy associated with larger-scale production.

### Content

Although prototypes are varied in type and nature, they share the commonality of being a model or mockup of the final deliverable. However, because they are models, rather than the real thing, some of their qualities will differ from the final deliverable. In order to present a prototype to an outside party, the project organization should ensure that the description of the prototype includes certain elements:

1. *Nature of the prototype.* What components, features, or elements of the real deliverable is the prototype supposed to emulate?
2. *Nonfunctional aspects of the prototype.* What components, features, or elements of the real deliverable will, by intent, be omitted from the prototype?
3. *Substitutions.* What elements of the real deliverable are not incorporated in the prototype, but instead have been replaced with a substitution for the sake of prototype development?
4. *Intent of the prototype.* What responses, inputs, and/or clarifications, are expected based on a review of the prototype?
5. *Iterations of the prototype.* Will only one prototype be developed or is the prototype one in a series of "draft" models that will be delivered prior to final production?

6. *Acceptable levels of change based on the prototype.* What should the reviewers be looking at/for? What are they allowed to change? Are there any aspects of the prototype that may not be changed?

## Approaches

The depth of information expected from a prototype review may range from a yes/no approval to an in-depth analysis of how the prototype looks, feels, or performs. Thus, the expectations for the prototype review should be clearly established. The more thoroughly the intent of the prototype and the acceptable level of change are detailed, the more likely the reviewers are to provide the information sought by the developing organization.

## Considerations

Prototypes are not the real thing. They do not function as the final deliverable, and there will always be some differences between a prototype and a final deliverable (even if they are simply differences in how they were produced). As such, reviewers need to be keenly aware of those differences, or they may cite those differences as "flaws" with the prototype. Prototypes also tend to be somewhat expensive, and reviewers also need to be aware of the limits to the number of iterative prototypes that will be developed before the deliverable goes into full, final production.

# Risk Assessment Form

## Purpose

Risk assessment forms are used to capture outputs from the risk management process so that key stakeholders are aware of both risks identified and the evaluations thereof. Some risk assessment forms are built with risk mitigation information as well, so as to track the responses and the outcomes of those responses. The risk assessment form is a component of a comprehensive risk archive. They may stand alone or be a component of a project status report.

## Application

Risk assessment forms are evolutionary documents, created at the beginning of the project, as individual risks are identified and then tracked through qualification and quantification. Risk assessment forms are used primarily to address the three steps of the risk process as outlined in the *Guide to the Project Management Body of Knowledge:* risk identification, risk qualification, and risk quantification [1]. The forms ensure that all identified risks are visible and that there is a consistent understanding as to the level of exposure that those risks create.

## Content

A risk assessment form will include the name and nature of the risk and any associated historical information. It should describe the risk event in depth and in sufficient detail that the exposure created by the risk can be readily understood by anyone who understands the nature of the project. The risk event should be stated as a complete sentence and should be expressed in terms of the causal factors, the event that may occur, and the impact of that event should it actually come to pass. In addition to the risk description, relative levels of probability and impact should also be included. Probability may be expressed either as a quantitative (percentage) value or as a value relative to other risks on the project (high, medium, low). Impact should be addressed based on the nature of the impact, because some risks are financial, while others may affect the schedule or the project's political standing. The content can be embodied in any software package with table or spreadsheet capability. In some environments, where risk response is handled separately from risk assessment, only the first five columns in Table 5.6 may be included.

## Approaches

The risk assessment form may be directly linked to the work breakdown structure, identifying a specific risk associated with each activity in the WBS. In such cases, the WBS code number for the deliverable or task may become the risk event number, as well. This becomes challenging in environments where some of the tasks have significant numbers of risks and others are relatively risk free.

## Considerations

Proper completion of a risk assessment form is predicated on the notion that there is a common understanding of the terms associated with risk management as it is practiced within the organization. If terms such as *high probability* or *medium impact* are arbitrarily assigned, it will be difficult for stakeholders to determine if a risk is truly worth responding to.

Assigning a single owner to each risk is also a key consideration, in that risks with multiple owners may not be addressed (because each owner believes the other to be truly responsible), and risks with no owners will generally fall back on the project manager, who is by nature fully engaged in other project activity.

**Table 5.6**  Sample Risk Assessment Form

| Risk Number | Risk Event | Probability | Impact | Overall Rating/ Priority | Response Strategy | Owner | Outcome |
|---|---|---|---|---|---|---|---|
| This may be a number specifically assigned to this risk event or one that ties the event to other project activity. | Stated as a full sentence, this is a description of the event that may occur and the causal or environmental factors. | This is the likelihood of occurrence, stated as a numeric value or as a relative (high–medium–low) term. | This is the severity if the risk comes to pass, stated as a numeric value or as a relative (high–medium–low) term. | This parameter is a function of probability times impact or other valuation system that is used to create a relative rank or priority. | This is a clearly stated plan for responding to the risk, even if the plan is one of "no action required." | This column lists the individual responsible for ensuring implementation of the response strategy. | This column lists the final dispensation of the risk event or response strategy. |

# Risk Log

## Purpose

The risk log is closely related to the risk assessment form, with the difference being that it is designed to monitor those risks that are under active scrutiny and allow for an at-a-glance view of their current status. The risk log is a list of high-priority risks, probability, impact, responses, and owners; it is coupled with the current status of those risk events and presented in a single table or view.

## Application

The risk log is used to present information to stakeholders on high-priority risk events and to allow for quick evaluation of where the project stands in terms of those risks. It can be used by the project manager to ensure that high-priority risks are being addressed and by management to ascertain if the responses to the most worrisome risks are, in their perception, adequate.

## Content

The content, look and feel of the table used for a risk log is not radically different from a risk assessment form, as demonstrated in Table 5.7. The only significant visible difference is in the last column, which addresses current status. One difference not visible in the sample table is that the risk log generally addresses only those risks that would be high priority and undergoing active consideration.

## Approaches

Because the risk assessment form and risk log are tightly linked, many of the cells in the table can be linked by the software packages so that a change in one drives a change in the other. That can facilitate any efforts to filter the table to show only current, high-priority risks and to update that status in real time, based on current owners, strategies, and descriptions.

**Table 5.7**   Sample Risk Log

| Risk Number | Risk Event | Probability | Impact | Overall Rating/ Priority | Response Strategy | Owner | Current Status |
|---|---|---|---|---|---|---|---|
| This may be a number specifically assigned to this risk event or one that ties the event to other project activity. | Stated as a full sentence, this is a description of the event that may occur and the causal or environmental factors. | This is the likelihood of occurrence, stated as a numeric value or as a relative (high– medium– low) term. | This is the severity if the risk comes to pass, stated as a numeric value or as a relative (high– medium– low) term. | This parameter is a function of probability times impact or other valuation system that is used to create a relative rank or priority. | This is a clearly stated plan for responding to the risk, even if the plan is one of "no action required." | This column lists the individual responsible for ensuring implementation of the response strategy. | This column lists whatever actions are under way or anticipated to be needed to deal with this risk. It also lists any shifts in probability or impact. |

### Considerations

Because some organizations are inherently form averse, it may be worthwhile to choose between the risk assessment form and the risk log or to generate an amalgam of the two.

## Technical Documents

### Purpose

Technical documents have a wide range of uses and, as such, they have a wide range of purposes. However, they share the common mission of being designed to convey, store and reproduce technical information for a technical audience. By virtue of their common audience and goals, some specific common approaches can be applied.

### Application

Technical documents are used in any environment where complex technical information needs to be shared. They should not be applied in environments where general information is required or where detailed information is needed by nontechnical personnel.

### Content

Again, because of the varied nature of technical document types, the content will vary widely. The content should be structured somewhat consistently, opening with a clear overview of the information included and an explanation of the technical background essential to a reasonable understanding of that content. The document should also include version control information, including the original date of creation, date of the most recent update, and the author(s)/reviser(s) of the document. Beyond that introductory information, the technical nature of the document will drive the content.

### Approaches

Some measure of consistency can be achieved by creating a common cover page or opening information table for all project technical documentation. That table should be formatted to apply to the range of technical documents the project organization needs to serve. A sample is shown in Table 5.8.

In this type of approach, the cover sheet or introductory table becomes a valuable document in and of itself, in that it provides the history of revisions for the document, the changes, and the sources of authority for those changes.

### Considerations

Some technical documentation authors will balk at the notion that they are required to track every iteration of their documentation. However, if that information can be developed consistently and is required of all technical document authors, resistance tends to be minimized. Also, the means for storage and transmission of any technical documentation need to be considered in its creation. If the document is to be stored

**Table 5.8**  Sample Technical Document Cover Page

| TECHNICAL DOCUMENT NAME: | | | | CODE #: |
|---|---|---|---|---|
| Nature of the document: | | | | |
| Technical expertise/background required: | | | | |
| DOCUMENT CREATED | By: | Contact information: | Date: | For project: |
| DOCUMENT REVISED | By: | Contact information: | Date: | By authority of: |
| DOCUMENT REVISED | By: | Contact information: | Date: | By authority of: |
| DOCUMENT REVISED | By: | Contact information: | Date: | By authority of: |
| DOCUMENT ARCHIVED | By: | Contact information: | Date: | Location: |

on the LAN, the repository should be consistent for all project documentation. If the document is to be stored in a physical file, the repository needs to be consistent, as well. That location needs to be communicated to project team members (as appropriate) to ensure that others can identify where the documentation is stored and can gain access to it as needed.

# Telephone Logs

### Purpose

Just as phone calls are intended for the quick transfer of information with some measure of immediacy, the telephone log is intended for quick documentation of what transpired in those telephone calls.

### Application

Phone calls are used liberally in modern business, but should be limited to those situations where an extensive documentary record is not essential or where time is of the essence. That said, the one tool that can provide a reasonable ongoing documentary record of phone calls is a telephone log. The telephone log, used effectively, is updated every time a telephone call is received.

### Content

Telephone logs detail the highlights of telephone call times, callers, and subject matter. They do not normally incorporate the details of the call, except to identify any specific promises or action items that were a result of the conversation.

A telephone log is normally maintained in a PDA or in a small, pocket-size note-book, and includes the headings shown in Table 5.9.

### Approaches

Consistency is the key for telephone logs, because ongoing maintenance of the telephone log record ensures credibility that all germane conversations have been tracked and documented. A spotty telephone record can easily be challenged as invalid on the basis that it is incomplete.

### Considerations

Phone logs are normally personal, rather than project, records but may be used as evidence of promises, commitments, and shared information. As a personal record, owners may be tempted to record information in their personal "shorthand" or note-taking method. As part of the project record, such stylized notes may be deemed invalid or unacceptable.

## Work Results

### Purpose

Work results are the output of any project effort. The documentation for work results is a record that the effort has been completed and the output has been produced. It is used as proof that the effort was put forth. As with technical documents, work results are used for a wide variety of purposes associated with the varied nature of the work that was completed.

### Application

Documentation from work results is used as affirmation that work has been accomplished as prescribed. If work was completed in a way other than how it was originally specified, the work results documentation will reflect that variance. The documentation is used as a tool to build evidence that progress is being made, that deliverables are being produced, and that effort is being put forth. At the work package level, that information allows the project manager to build a piece-by-piece history of project progress. At the summary levels, that information can be presented to management or the customer to highlight the volume and nature of work accomplished.

**Table 5.9**   Sample Telephone Log

| Date/Time | Initiator | Caller | Subject Matter | Promises/Action Items | Follow-Up Date(s) |
|---|---|---|---|---|---|
| The date and time the call occurred | A simple "me" or "them" to identify who called whom | Name and contact telephone of caller | Topic of conversation | Specific promises or action items planned as a result | Time reference for any requisite follow-up conversation |

### Content

The work results documentation content will vary somewhat, based on the type of work that has been accomplished. The content should be structured consistently, however, to ensure ease of understanding and use. The documentation should include the original requirement, any coding or numbering for that requirement, the start and finish dates for the effort, the owner of the activity, contact information for the owner, and the status or dispensation of the final deliverable or output.

### Approaches

The work results documentation may be attached directly to the work output itself. Thus, the documentation may serve as a cover page or introductory table for that information, as illustrated in Table 5.10.

### Considerations

There is a temptation on some "lesser" activities (including many administrative functions) to overlook or forego this type of documentation. That's understandable, because it is an administrative effort in itself. However, it is precisely those types of activities that may be addressed most effectively by this type of data capture, since it may highlight work that was not required, variance that has not been addressed, or lesser levels of effort that have been overlooked or dropped.

## Conclusion

During execution, project managers may become so overwhelmed with the volume of work and the level of activity that organizational practice can easily be forgotten. Thus, the forms and formats included herein often serve to preserve the process by virtue of their adherence to rote performance of basic reporting, tracking, and information storage tasks. As with all of the components in this book, the key is consistency. The more consistent project managers become in their management of communications and information, the more effective they are.

**Table 5.10**   Sample Work Result Cover Page

| Work Result | | | | |
|---|---|---|---|---|
| Requirement number: | Requirement (citation from memorandum of understanding or contract) | WBS Code: | Activity/summary (citation from work breakdown structure) | |
| Date required | | Dates | Start: | Finish: |
| Requirement owner | | Contact information | | |
| Activity owner (if different) | | Contact information | | |
| Variance assessment | | | | |
| Was there variance? | Yes: ☐  No: ☐ | If yes, define the nature: | | |
| Current Status | | | | |

# Reference

[1]    *Guide to the Project Management Body of Knowledge,* Newton Square, PA: Project Management Institute, 2000.

## CHAPTER 6

# Communications Tools in the Controlling Processes

Controlling is what project managers do to ensure that what was promised is what is delivered. Controlling tools are those tools that allow the project manager, the team, and senior management to see how the project is doing, what directions it may be taking, and how those directions may affect the individuals, the project(s), and the organizations involved. Many of the tools and templates in this book serve the controlling processes in one way or another, because they ultimately provide the project manager with tools to compare what was promised to what is actually happening on the project.

## Control Book

### Purpose

The project control book is designed to present information on what the project organization is delivering or has delivered and details the ways in which those deliverables are presented (as well as their final location and dispensation). It is used in environments where high levels of requirements detail are required and where multiple audiences need to review or understand that detail.

### Application

Project control books are used to capture and catalog forms, formats, and locations and to clearly define what requirements have been met and the ways in which they were met. It is developed as early in the project as possible, evolving with new documentation and data as the project progresses. As a document to support transition of deliverables to the customer, the project control book can be invaluable, because it provides both structure and history for the project deliverables.

### Content

The project control book includes a general scope statement for the project, as well as a statement regarding the scope of the control book itself. That statement defines what information is included in the control book and what information is not. The control book also includes a glossary of terms and acronyms germane to the project and the supporting organizations. Some control books will incorporate an extensive list of reference materials (and the locations of those materials). The bulk of the control book, however, focuses on the project deliverables and the components of those deliverables. It goes into excruciating detail about how the deliverables are to be used, applied, or integrated into the client environment and how and where the deliverables are formatted and stored.

The outline for the project control book may appear as follows:

1.0   Scope of the Project
2.0   Scope of the Document
3.0   Related Documentation
4.0   Overview of the Deliverables
  4.1   Integrated
  4.2   Components
5.0   Deliverable Detail
  5.1   Component #1
    5.1.1   Form/structure
    5.1.2   Format
    5.1.3   Use
    5.1.4   Storage/dispensation
  5.2   Component #2
    5.2.1   Form/structure
    5.2.2   …
6.0   Supporting Information
  6.1   Reference materials
  6.2   Glossary of terms and acronyms
7.0   Document Ownership
  7.1   Author(s)/contact information
  7.2   Archivist(s)/contact information
8.0   Document information
  8.1   Most recent date amended
  8.2   Version/configuration coding (if applicable)
  8.3   Distribution

## Approaches

The control book may be developed either in hard copy or virtually, and it generally evolves as the project deliverables evolve. It is not created at the end of the project, because that could lead to missed components or data elements. Each time a new component of the deliverable is generated, a new page (temporary or permanent) is added to the project control book.

## Considerations

Control books grew out of the software industry, which had a serious need to track data formats and to monitor the slightest changes in configuration. This level of detail is appropriate in any environment where configuration is the key to a successful customer handoff. If the customer must integrate multiple systems or products with a deliverable, the information provided in a control book can prove invaluable. However, if the deliverable is a stand-alone product with limited need for customer integration, a control book can be potentially self-defeating for the project organization. The control book may give up some information that represents key intellectual property for the project organization. In the process, it may also facilitate reverse engineering of the deliverables, allowing the customer to see the intricate details of what went into the deliverables' construction.

## Dashboard Report

### Purpose

The dashboard report is a report to senior management that provides an at-a-glance perspective on the current status of the project in the context of predetermined metrics for that project. Depending on the organization, those metrics may include cost, time, requirements, risk, customer satisfaction, or other measures critical to the management team. It provides management with a quick understanding of the current project posture, without a detailed explanation of the causes or solutions.

### Application

In organizations where multiple projects limit the amount of management involvement, dashboard reports are used to allow managers and executives to examine and assess project status. It facilitates discussion by highlighting only metric status points, encouraging management by exception, where deviations from the norm become the focal points of discussion. Those metrics should be established early in the project and applied as the project takes form.

### Content

A dashboard report relies on metric content built on detailed reporting from the project team and the project manager. Dashboard reports frequently include earned value data, including the value of the work completed to date (earned value), the amount of work scheduled to date (planned value), and the actual costs. With those metrics and the overall project budget, basic information regarding schedule variance, cost variance, and updated estimates at completion may be generated. Other metrics may include:

- Number of change requests;
- Staff overtime;
- Team member loss/turnover;
- Defect rates;
- Risk reserve consumed;
- New high-impact risks identified;
- Anything else that can be measured by the numbers.

Dashboard reports often include graphs and graphics that quickly highlight where there are concerns, as well as the degree of those concerns.

### Approaches

As the name implies, the dashboard report often takes on the look and feel of an instrument panel in a car or plane. It is a set of graphic representations of the metric information of importance to management, as shown in Figure 6.1. In this example, the dashboard indicates a negative cost variance, a positive schedule variance, and quite a few outstanding high-impact risks. It also illustrates that, although overall change requests are not straying into dangerous territory, this month's level of change requests was venturing into a zone considered unacceptable (for this time period). The entire chart is designed for "at-a-glance" reviews.

### Considerations

Perhaps the greatest danger associated with dashboard reports is that management may believe they understand the intricacies of the project by virtue of this limited amount of information. They sometimes must be reminded that reading a dashboard report no more makes one aware of the details of a project than reading the indicators on a car's dashboard makes one a mechanic. It's a quick, effective overview of critical metrics.

## Earned Value Analysis

### Purpose

Earned value analyses provide status reports on project performance presented in the context of time and money. Normally generated within project management software, earned value analysis generates perspectives on the time and cost status of the work package and summary and project levels of the WBS, allowing for pinpoint assessments of where cost overruns and schedule delays are being generated.

### Application

Earned value analyses are normally used on larger dollar-value efforts where actual costs are being tracked and where individual employee allocations are loaded into the specific work packages. Earned value may be applied on smaller efforts if the tracking mechanisms are in place for both effort and actual costs at the project level. The analyses are used to assess relative cost and schedule variance, as well as to predict the future cost and schedule performance, based on performance to date.

### Content

Earned value reports include a variety of information elements, presented in a spreadsheet format, juxtaposed with the WBS (Table 6.1). Those elements normally include (at least) the following:

- *Earned value (EV)*. Also known as the *budgeted cost of work performed* (BCWP), earned value is the dollar value that was originally budgeted for the level of effort completed on a task or project to date.

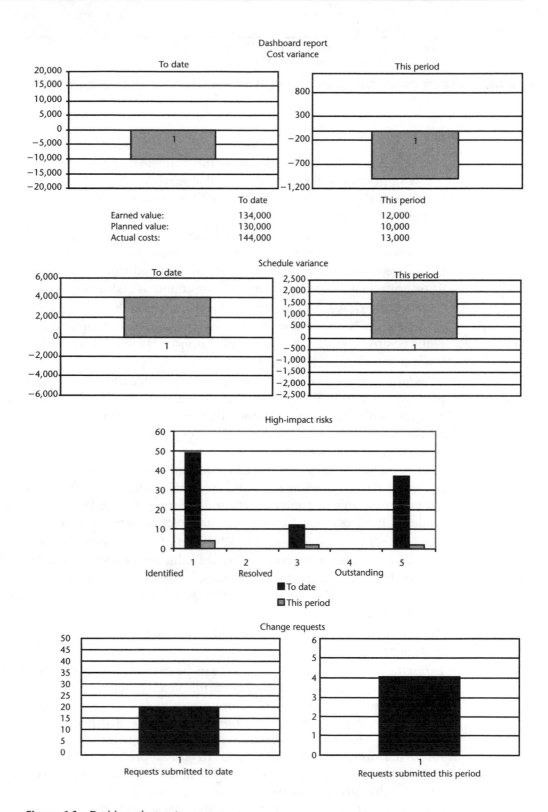

**Figure 6.1** Dashboard report.

**Table 6.1**  Earned Value Analysis

| Task/Summary/ Project Identifier | Earned Value | Planned Value | Actual Costs | Cost Variance | Schedule Variance | CPI | SPI | BAC | EAC |
|---|---|---|---|---|---|---|---|---|---|
|  |  |  |  |  |  |  |  |  |  |

- *Planned value (PV)*. Also known as the *budgeted cost of work scheduled* (BCWS), planned value is the dollar value that was originally budgeted as of the date of the assessment, regardless of how much (or how little) work has actually be accomplished.
- *Actual costs (AC)*. Also known as the *actual cost of work performed* (ACWP), actual costs are what the name implies. They are the costs that have actually been invested on the project. They are not derived from plans or formulas. They are actual monies spent on the project and/or tasks.
- *Cost variance (CV)*. This is calculated by subtracting the actual costs from the earned value. Negative cost variance in earned value indicates cost overruns, while positive cost variance indicates that more work has been performed for less money.
- *Schedule variance (SV)*. Schedule variance is calculated by subtracting the planned value from the earned value. A negative schedule variance indicates that less work has been performed than was scheduled, whereas a positive schedule variance indicates that more work has been performed than was scheduled to be performed.
- *Cost performance index (CPI)*. CPI is an indicator of relative cost performance, calculated by dividing actual costs by the earned value. A CPI of greater than 1.0 indicates that the project (or activity) is costing less than expected, while a CPI of less than 1.0 indicates that costs are greater than budgeted.
- *Schedule performance index (SPI)*. SPI is an indicator of relative schedule performance, calculated by dividing planned value by the earned value. An SPI of greater than 1.0 indicates that more work has been performed than was scheduled, whereas an SPI of less than 1.0 indicates that less work has been performed than was scheduled.
- *Budget at completion (BAC)*. The budget at completion is the total budgeted cost for the project.
- *Estimate at completion (EAC)*. EAC can be calculated in a variety of ways, depending on the nature of project performance to date. If project performance to date is an indicator of future performance, the EAC may be calculated by dividing the *budget at completion by the cost performance index* (BAC/CPI). The number generated will be the estimate for total project costs if future performance continues as it has to date. If project performance to date has not been normal (i.e., cost overruns or underruns are anomalous), the EAC can be calculated by taking the budget at completion and subtracting the earned value, then adding the actual costs. This second approach assumes that the budgeted funds will be adequate for the remainder of the project.

For all information, the sources of the data should be clear. For EAC, the calculation approach should be indicated.

### Approaches

The differences in approach on earned value stem largely from the "schools of thought" on how it should be practiced. Originally created in the U.S. Department of Defense, earned value in government organizations (and in many of the software packages) adheres to the older acronyms (BCWP, BCWS, ACWP) and to an environment where certain rules must be followed to receive credit for task completion (or partial completion).

Classic earned value simply multiplies a percentage of task completion by the total value of the task to calculate earned value (e.g., a task that is valued at $40,000 and is 25% complete would have earned value of $10,000). In some organizations, the 50–50 rule is applied, in which any task or work package that is under way is marked as 50% complete (e.g., a work package that is valued at $40,000 and is 25% complete would be marked as 50% complete and have earned value of $20,000). Any rules used to calculate earned value and to ensure it is applied consistently should be documented with the earned value analysis or tables.

### Considerations

One key consideration in earned value is the timing of the information provided. Because some information (particularly actual cost) is only available after a thorough accounting process has been conducted, the date of the earned value analysis may be days, or even weeks, in the past. For any earned value analysis, the data date (the effective date of the analysis) should be consistent for all components (earned value, planned value, actual costs). If the earned value is assessed as of today, and the actual costs are from several days ago, the comparison will be invalid.

## Issues List

### Purpose

The issues list is a list of concerns regarding the effect of the project on its environment and the effects of the environment on the project. It is used to alert project stakeholders to existing problems and, in some cases, to identify or catalog strategies for resolution of those problems.

### Application

The issues list is used to present the concerns of the project owners and the team in an open environment to encourage resolution of those concerns. It differs from a risk log (Chapter 5) in that an issues list highlights concerns that currently exist on a project, rather than those that may come to pass at some point in the future. Issues are problems. Issues are risks whose time has come.

The list becomes an archive of concerns about the project and its environment and the strategies that are deployed to contend with those concerns.

## Content

The issues list should include a clearly stated list of current concerns about the project, any identifying codes, owners, and dispensation, as shown in Table 6.2.

A key with issues lists is to ensure that they are seen as unbiased analyses of concerns that surround a project, rather than as opportunities to complain about the project, its stakeholders, or its environment.

## Approaches

Issues lists are normally stakeholder-generated documents and are available to the project owners through a common repository. That repository may be a poster in the project "war room" or a dedicated file on the LAN. Issues lists are normally constructed and reviewed in regular team meetings and are updated whenever new issues arise. They should be reviewed at regular intervals.

## Considerations

The issues list can become an area of contention in some organizations, because stakeholders sometimes use the issues list to identify what they perceive as shortcomings with other stakeholders on the project. It is up to the project manager (or the owner of the issues list) to ensure that the list maintains a somewhat sterile tone, identifying areas of concern without direct attribution of blame.

It is also important to ensure that team members know the differences between risks and issues, because issues require strategies that deal with their existence in the present, whereas risks require strategies that deal with the possibility that the risks may or may not come to pass.

# Meeting Minutes

## Purpose

Meeting minutes provide a narrative history of the suggestions, activities, and decisions made during a meeting. They also encompass a list of attendees, their roles, and the original agenda for the meeting.

**Table 6.2**  Sample Issues List

| ID | Issue | Strategy for Resolution | Owner | Next Review Date |
|---|---|---|---|---|
| Identifying code | Specific existing problem or area of concern, stated as a full sentence, including any primary sources of the issue or individuals/ organizations affected | Current plan to deal with the issue or to change the environment in which the issue exists | Name and contact information for the individual responsible | Date of next planned review |

## Application

Meeting minutes are used any time a formal meeting is held, particularly those meetings in which decisions are being made. They are used as background and history of the meeting should disputes arise about what was said during the meeting or who said it. Because they serve as a documented history, minutes are normally approved as authoritative or final in a later meeting.

## Content

Meeting minutes primarily consist of narrative regarding the activities that occurred during a specific meeting. A simple outline for meeting minutes would include the following:

1.0   Agenda
2.0   Attendees
  2.1   In person
  2.2   Teleconferenced/virtual
3.0   Discussion
4.0   Findings, Recommendations, and Action Items

The longest single component is normally the discussion element, which strives to capture the points and counterpoints that were made during the meeting. Without being a verbatim transcript, meeting minutes will identify who made what arguments or contentions during the meeting (e.g., "Wilbur Post suggested that sugar cubes might be an unnecessary expense and that the livestock would be just as healthy with a less elaborate diet.") The discussion will normally be outlined in the same fashion as the agenda (assuming the agenda was actually followed).

Findings, recommendations, and action items identify specific accomplishments in the meeting and how the meeting attendees determined those findings would be carried out. For action items, a specific owner is identified, as well.

## Approaches

Because minutes must reflect the give and take of a meeting and the statements of various participants, the insights should be developed in real time to ensure no loss of memory or information. Minutes are normally maintained by a single individual, who is ideally not a participating member of the meeting group. This individual's sole focus should be to capture the meeting minutes and to document the findings and action items. The minute-taker should also ensure that any highly charged discussions are muted to reflect only the information that was shared and the individual(s) who shared it.

## Considerations

Minutes are potentially politically charged documents in almost any environment. Because they become the history and the long-term perspective on what was said and who said it, minutes can skew the historical perspective. That's why it is important to have them reviewed and validated before they become authoritative. It is also important to ensure that the minute-taker knows his role in the process and understands the importance of ensuring a clear, honest record of the meeting.

## Performance Reports

### Purpose

Performance reports generate a mutually accepted understanding of how an individual, process, or deliverable is performing against a predetermined set of standards. Performance reports document the degree of acceptability of that performance and may include recommendations on how to improve performance.

### Application

In human resource applications, performance reports are used on a regular basis (monthly, quarterly, semiannually) to provide an assessment of how individuals are working toward their project or organizational objectives. In process or deliverable applications, performance reports are developed as the process or deliverable is implemented (and again at a predetermined interval) to ascertain how well the process or deliverable is meeting its objectives. Because the best performance reports are driven by preordained objective metrics, the report structure should be established as early in the process as possible.

Ideally, performance reports in either environment will clearly state the objective measures being evaluated and the degree to which those measures have been achieved.

### Content

#### Human Resources

A human resource performance report includes an assessment of the specific objectives the individual was to achieve and the degree to which those objectives were met. Table 6.3 provides a sample.

#### Process or Deliverable

In building the performance reports for a process or deliverable, the "objective" becomes an anticipated state of performance and, if that state is not achieved, rationales are provided as to how or why not. A sample process/deliverable report is shown in Table 6.4.

### Approaches

The emphasis on performance reports is the ability of the individual, process, or deliverable to meet desired standards or goals. Some may try to blend performance reports with progress reports, which are similar, but which focus on a gradient level of achievement, rather than objective, yes/no measures. Performance reports should be completed when a particular level of performance has been achieved or at the time at which that level of performance was anticipated.

### Considerations

One key consideration in developing performance reports is establishing the objective measures by which the individual or the deliverable will be assessed. While it is

**Table 6.3**  Sample Employee Performance Report

| *Employee Performance Report* | | | |
|---|---|---|---|
| Name: | | Employee Code: | |
| Objective | Objectives should be as unambiguous as possible to ensure that they can be documented as either met or unmet or so a degree of progress can clearly be assigned. | Date Assigned: | Date Reviewed: |
| | | Current Status: | Notes: |
| Objective | Objectives should be as unambiguous as possible to ensure that they can be documented as either met or unmet or so a degree of progress can clearly be assigned. | Date Assigned: | Date Reviewed: |
| | | Current Status: | Notes: |
| Objective | Objectives should be as unambiguous as possible to ensure that they can be documented as either met or unmet or so a degree of progress can clearly be assigned. | Date Assigned: | Date Reviewed: |
| | | Current Status: | Notes |
| Summary of Findings | | | |
| Date: | | | |

relatively easy to evaluate the performance of a process or person relative to other processes and people, it is far more challenging to find the specific metrics by which to validate those findings.

# Progress Report

### Purpose

Progress reports afford insight on the current standing of the project, as well as the effort taken to get it to its current state. They are used to provide interim updates to management, the customer, and the team regarding effort taken, accomplishments achieved, and shortcomings faced.

### Application

Progress reports are used to affirm to concerned stakeholders that work is actually being done on the project and that accomplishments are being made, particularly when such efforts may not be visible at a surface level. Some types of progress reports are called for within contractual arrangements, while others are completed under mandates of organizational protocol. They should be used to present an honest assessment of the effort undertaken, the comparison of that effort with the effort anticipated, the deliverables produced, and the comparison of those deliverables

**Table 6.4**   Sample Process/Deliverable Performance Report

| *Process/Deliverable Performance Report* | | | |
|---|---|---|---|
| Process under review: | | Functional area: | |
| Desired state | As with objectives, these should be as unambiguous as possible to ensure that they can be documented as either met or unmet or so a degree of progress can clearly be assigned. | Date Assigned: | Date Reviewed: |
| | | Current Status: | Rationale If Not Achieved: |
| Desired state | As with objectives, these should be as unambiguous as possible to ensure that they can be documented as either met or unmet or so a degree of progress can clearly be assigned. | Date Assigned: | Date Reviewed: |
| | | Current Status: | Rationale If Not Achieved: |
| Desired state | As with objectives, these should be as unambiguous as possible to ensure that they can be documented as either met or unmet or so a degree of progress can clearly be assigned. | Date Assigned: | Date Reviewed: |
| | | Current Status: | Rationale If Not Achieved: |
| Summary of Findings | | | |
| Date: | | | |
| Author/Reviewer: | | | |

with the deliverables promised and to reflect on the challenges and opportunities that surfaced during those experiences.

### Content

Progress reports take a wide variety of forms, including some that are nothing more than earned value analyses. For the sake of clarity, however, a progress report should be a succinct discussion that takes into account the intended path of the project and how work has progressed along (or divergent from) that path. The progress report should highlight major accomplishments (if practical) and should provide some space for narrative analysis of the effort to date.

### Approaches

One approach to a progress report is to make it a comprehensive review of all aspects of the project, with ample space for commentary, as illustrated in Table 6.5.

Another approach to the progress report is much closer to simple status reporting and involves listing the critical project milestones and providing insight on the progress made toward achieving them, as shown in the list in Table 6.6. Notable in its absence in this table is a reference to "work performed." The assumption in a checklist this voluminous is that the work will be reflected in status reports mapped to the work breakdown structure.

**Table 6.5**  Sample Progress Report

| *Progress Report* | | | | | |
|---|---|---|---|---|---|
| Project Name: | | Project Manager: | | Progress Report Date: | |
| **Project Summary Information** | | | | | |
| Project Start Date | | Original Planned Completion | | Revised Completion Date | Next Schedule Review Date |
| Project Total Budget | | Project Contingency | | Contingency Consumed | Target Final Cost |

Executive Summary:
Highlights here should include significant individual and team accomplishments, as well as a summary of why schedule and/or cost variances may exist. Any customer concerns should be incorporated here as well.

Project Detail Information (activity in process or recently completed)

| Deliverable/ Activity | Scheduled Start | Planned Completion | Actual Start | Revised Completion | Rationale |
|---|---|---|---|---|---|
| | | | | | |
| | | | | | |

Risk Update

| New Risk Identified | Probability | Impact | Response Strategy | Owner | Status/Outcome |
|---|---|---|---|---|---|
| | | | | | |
| | | | | | |

| Existing Risk Modified | Probability | Impact | Response | Owner | Nature of Change/ Status |
|---|---|---|---|---|---|
| | | | | | |
| | | | | | |

Additional Comments/Notes:

## Considerations

One of the keys of effective progress reporting is to provide data at the depth to which it is truly required. There is often a temptation to provide more information than is required simply because the information may be available. Some managers may thrive on such torrents of data, but others will find themselves awash in it. It is up to the project manager to ascertain the appropriate level of reporting, but once such a level has been agreed on, it should be continued at that level for the duration of the project. It is equally important to note that some senior managers will use the progress report as an opportunity to micromanage the project by requesting more data. That should also be a consideration in establishing the appropriate level of depth for the information provided.

**Table 6.6**   Sample of a Status-Type Progress Report

| *Concept Phase* | |
| --- | --- |
| ☐ Project manager assigned | Date delivered or rationale for nonuse: |
| ☐ Project sponsor assigned | Date delivered or rationale for nonuse: |
| ☐ Project charter drafted (using charter template) | Date delivered or rationale for nonuse: |
| ☐ Project charter approved | Date delivered or rationale for nonuse: |
| *Development Phase* | |
| ☐ Project kickoff meeting held | Date delivered or rationale for nonuse: |
| ☐ First draft WBS completed | Date delivered or rationale for nonuse: |
| ☐ Budget estimate created | Date delivered or rationale for nonuse: |
| ☐ Responsibility matrix created | Date delivered or rationale for nonuse: |
| ☐ Team rules established | Date delivered or rationale for nonuse: |
| ☐ Communications plan circulated | Date delivered or rationale for nonuse: |
| ☐ Issues resolution procedures created | Date delivered or rationale for nonuse: |
| ☐ Resource roles drafted | Date delivered or rationale for nonuse: |
| ☐ Initial risk identification conducted | Date delivered or rationale for nonuse: |
| ☐ Initial risk analysis/prioritization conducted | Date delivered or rationale for nonuse: |
| ☐ Project plan and schedule created | Date delivered or rationale for nonuse: |
| ☐ Change management procedures created | Date delivered or rationale for nonuse: |
| ☐ Milestone schedule established | Date delivered or rationale for nonuse: |
| ☐ Project environment reviewed | Date delivered or rationale for nonuse: |
| ☐ Deliverables schedule established | Date delivered or rationale for nonuse: |
| ☐ Quality control plan created | Date delivered or rationale for nonuse: |
| ☐ Functional requirements reviewed | Date delivered or rationale for nonuse: |
| ☐ Technical requirements finalized | Date delivered or rationale for nonuse: |
| ☐ Training requirements established | Date delivered or rationale for nonuse: |

**Table 6.6** (Continued)

| | |
|---|---|
| ☐ Stakeholder analysis developed | Date delivered or rationale for nonuse: |
| ☐ Project plan documentation compiled | Date delivered or rationale for nonuse: |
| ☐ Project process/template documents created | Date delivered or rationale for nonuse: |
| ☐ Time tracking established | Date delivered or rationale for nonuse: |
| ☐ Deliverables/production checklist created | Date delivered or rationale for nonuse: |
| ☐ Implementation plan finalized | Date delivered or rationale for nonuse: |
| ☐ Specifications generated | Date delivered or rationale for nonuse: |
| ☐ Requirements document finalized and signatures attained | Date delivered or rationale for nonuse: |
| ☐ Analysis and design documents generated | Date delivered or rationale for nonuse: |
| ☐ Equipment purchased | Date delivered or rationale for nonuse: |
| ☐ Vendor support purchased | Date delivered or rationale for nonuse: |
| ☐ Requirements review conducted | Date delivered or rationale for nonuse: |
| ☐ Resource allocation reviewed | Date delivered or rationale for nonuse: |
| ☐ Project-specific training identified | Date delivered or rationale for nonuse: |
| ☐ Project documentation needs identified | Date delivered or rationale for nonuse: |
| *Project Implementation* | |
| ☐ Final authorization received | Date delivered or rationale for nonuse: |
| ☐ Acceptance criteria finalized | Date delivered or rationale for nonuse: |
| ☐ Final work plan (WBS) generated | Date delivered or rationale for nonuse: |
| ☐ Interim review/audit planned | Date delivered or rationale for nonuse: |
| ☐ Interim review/audit conducted | Date delivered or rationale for nonuse: |
| ☐ Project authorization documents posted | Date delivered or rationale for nonuse: |
| ☐ Trainers identified | Date delivered or rationale for nonuse: |
| ☐ Functional managers identified and contacted | Date delivered or rationale for nonuse: |
| ☐ Customer acceptance received | Date delivered or rationale for nonuse: |

**Table 6.6**　(Continued)

| | |
|---|---|
| ☐ Project final audit conducted | Date delivered or rationale for nonuse: |
| ☐ Operations handoff document created | Date delivered or rationale for nonuse: |
| ☐ Operations and support personnel trained | Date delivered or rationale for nonuse: |
| ☐ Acceptance signatures received at all levels | Date delivered or rationale for nonuse: |
| *Project Control* | |
| ☐ Status meetings conducted | Date(s) delivered or rationale for nonuse: |
| ☐ Sponsor meetings established and conducted | Date(s) delivered or rationale for nonuse: |
| ☐ Budgeting documents generated | Date delivered or rationale for nonuse: |
| ☐ Escalation procedures document generated | Date delivered or rationale for nonuse: |
| ☐ Change control procedures implemented | Date delivered or rationale for nonuse: |
| ☐ Action item documents maintained | Date(s) delivered or rationale for nonuse: |
| ☐ Project timeline updates completed | Date(s) delivered or rationale for nonuse: |
| ☐ Monthly status reports generated | Date(s) delivered or rationale for nonuse: |
| *Project Termination* | |
| ☐ Final output document generated | Date delivered or rationale for nonuse: |
| ☐ Customer satisfaction survey developed | Date delivered or rationale for nonuse: |
| ☐ Customer satisfaction survey received and tallied | Date delivered or rationale for nonuse: |
| ☐ Lessons learned meeting conducted | Date delivered or rationale for nonuse: |
| ☐ Lessons learned documentation generated and archived | Date delivered or rationale for nonuse: |
| ☐ Final plan updated | Date delivered or rationale for nonuse: |
| ☐ Sponsor review conducted | Date delivered or rationale for nonuse: |
| ☐ Project completion report drafted | Date delivered or rationale for nonuse: |
| ☐ Documents filed | Date delivered or rationale for nonuse: |
| ☐ Project data archived | Date delivered or rationale for nonuse: |
| ☐ Final resource reallocation and time justification conducted | Date delivered or rationale for nonuse: |

## Recovery Plan

### Purpose

The recovery plan is intended to provide a clear direction for getting a project that has strayed from its initial approach and objectives back to where there is a means to deliver either all or part of the original project intent. It is designed to ensure that a direction is in place that can still provide some level of customer satisfaction with the project outputs. It may or may not be designed to return the project to the original plan. If the original plan is no longer reasonable or valid, the recovery plan may take an entirely new approach to the work.

### Application

Recovery plans are applied when a project has strayed from its ability to serve the basic project objectives. They are used as an alternative or last resort, since by their nature, they represent a new approach to doing the work and mean that some of the effort to date probably was conducted in the wrong direction. Project recovery plans may be generated at the request of the customer, as a response to a cure notice or other admonition that the project is not progressing in line with expectations.

### Content

Because the causes of project failure are legion, the content of recovery plans may take many different forms, but will normally address the failures to date in terms of the triple constraint. That is, the project may be failing to meet schedule objectives, cost objectives, scope objectives, or any combination of the three. A recovery plan will incorporate the type of information discussed in the following subsections.

#### 1.0   General Project Objective and Overview

The overview is a simple restatement of the project intent and the project team's approach to serving that intent. It may even be directly copied from the original scope statement.

#### 2.0   Current Project Status

The project status section identifies the specific project shortcomings in terms of the triple constraint and performance within that constraint. The information included herein may be drawn directly from progress or status reports.

#### 3.0   Nature of the Concern

This section reflects the specific customer or project team concerns that led to the conclusion that the existing plan would no longer serve to achieve the project's triple constraint objectives. It should provide detail on the depth of the concern and any environmental factors that are contributing to the project team's inability to use the existing plan to achieve the intended goals.

4.0   Recovery Overview

*4.1   Approach*   The approach section provides a basic assessment of how the project will be brought back in line with its original objective. It is comparable to a new scope statement for the remaining work.

*4.2   Work Activities*   Work activities are the activities required to accomplish the new scope, including any explanation necessary on how or why they support the objectives more effectively than the activities applied in the original project approach.

*4.3   Environmental Factors*   Environmental factors are the conditions in the project surroundings that may directly influence the ability to achieve the project objective but that are not specifically tied to work performance or team member capability. They are included in the recovery plan to ensure that all parties are aware of the assumptions regarding the environment, so that if those assumptions vary, there is an understanding that the capability to produce project deliverables may vary as well.

*4.4   Work Sequence*   The work sequence section covers the rescheduling of work, milestones, and deliverables in such a way that if progress and/or performance payments are tied to those milestones, they are identified within the new approach.

*4.5   Cost Considerations*   Particularly in cost reimbursement contracts, any shifts in project reporting approaches or capabilities must be noted. Because the recovery plan may involve extensive additional cost, there should be a shared, documented understanding of who will bear the burden for such costs.

*4.6   Rationale*   Because the original approach was unsuccessful, some defense for the new approach is included to reassure all parties that the new tactics will be more successful than the original ones.

*4.7   Signatures*   All those who authorized the original project plan (and are still active project participants) should sign the recovery plan. Their authorization serves as an affirmation that this plan supersedes the original and is now the official plan of record.

## Approaches

The recovery plan is, by its nature, an admission of failed planning for the original project plan. As such, the authors of the recovery plan need to openly document why the previous approach was not successful and why the updated approach should be. It should be built with the same level of rigor (if not more) as the original project plan and should include the trappings of an updated schedule, an updated budget, and an updated scope statement. All of these elements should be present, even if only one aspect of the project is in question. For example, if schedule delays have stretched to almost double the project length, the updated budget and scope statements are still important, because they are inherently tied to the organization's ability to achieve a time target. Once approved and signed, the recovery plan should supplant all existing copies of the project plan, and the original project plan should be set aside as an historic document.

### Considerations

Because recovery plans are tied to failure, there is a temptation to ascribe blame for past problems in the new plan. A recovery plan should be candid in discussing existing project problems, but should not focus on individuals. The true focus of the recovery plan is moving the project forward toward its objectives and ensuring that all stakeholders are in concurrence that the new approach can serve the objectives far more effectively than the approach that had been used to date.

## RYG Tool

### Purpose

The RYG (red–yellow–green) tool is used for management or customer reporting to provide an at-a-glance overview of areas of concern and areas where there are no concerns. The RYG tools (also known as a red–amber–green, or RAG, tools) give managers the means to evaluate overall status, as well as the status of specific elements or components of the project.

### Application

RYG tools are used by project managers who want to provide more general, rather than specific, information about project or activity status. They are frequently used in project environments where multiple projects or programs render in-depth analysis by senior management either impossible or extremely challenging. They can be used either as status reporting tools for specific project activities or deliverables or as status reporting tools for issue management or risk management.

### Content

RYG tools are made up of list of project elements (activities, deliverables, risks, or issues) and a corresponding color dot for each (Table 6.7). Additional information may be provided to explain why a particular element is endangered and how the problem may ultimately be resolved. The tools also incorporate legends to explain the specific criteria applied to determine why a red (danger), yellow (caution), or green (all clear) dot is appropriate. In some organizations, because of color printing limitations, the color description is also incorporated below the dot.

The greatest level of detail is embedded in the legends that accompany these tools. For an activity or deliverable RYG tool, the legend might read as follows:

**Table 6.7**   Sample RYG Tool

| Project Element (Activity, Deliverable, Risk, Issue) | RYG Status | Rationale and Recovery Plan (R or Y only) |
|---|---|---|
|  | O Red/Yellow/Green |  |

- Red indicates that the activity's planned completion date is greater than X days beyond its originally scheduled date or the budget targets for the task may be exceeded (or have been exceeded) by more than 15%. Red may also indicate that the task cannot be performed as originally intended.
- Yellow (amber) indicates that the activity's planned completion date may slip, but it is unlikely it will be delayed by X days or more. It may also indicate budget targets that have or may be exceeded, but by less than 15%. Yellow may also indicate that the task may face unforeseen technical challenges, but they may be overcome.
- Green indicates the activity has no significant time, cost, or scope issues.

For a risk or issues RYG tool, the legend might read this way:

- Red indicates that there is a risk or issue requiring direct intervention of the customer or senior management that is outside the purview or control of the project manager. It may also indicate risks that are imminent and are outside the purview or control of all project parties.
- Yellow (amber) indicates that the project manager and team are mitigating or accepting significant risk, but that their efforts do not require direct management intervention at this time.
- Green indicates that the risks and/or issues are either within acceptable thresholds or that the existing mitigation or resolution strategies are sound and functioning as planned.

In either environment, the intent is to give management the ability to quickly sort and assess the number and type of major concerns.

### Approaches

The RYG tool is particularly effective in environments where management must have the ability to do a quick, scanning review of project information. Thus, the tool is often built in a spreadsheet program to allow for automatic filtering of the information by color or by grouping of project elements.

### Considerations

Some organizations build RYG practices into their regular status reporting without legends, allowing the project managers to establish the color coding at their discretion. That's a very dangerous practice, in that different project managers will have radically different tolerances for delays, cost overruns, and risk. The most effective practices are those that are applied consistently.

## Status Meeting Agenda

### Purpose

Project status meetings are designed to share information about project performance to date and to ensure that team members are communicating about their respective needs and integrated functions. The agenda for such meetings serve to communicate the timing and approach to serve those functions.

## Application

The agenda should be delivered to all participants at least a day in advance of the meeting to allow for proper preparation and to ensure that any sensitive agenda items can be identified (and, in some cases, resolved) prior to the meeting. Project status meetings are conducted at regular intervals to affirm that the project is in control and that progress is being made according to the plan. This makes developing the agenda easier, because the meetings are expected on a regular basis.

## Content

The agenda for a status meeting normally consists of a breakdown of the project into logical components. Therefore, the meeting may be divided according to the schedule, the WBS, or the organizational functions. For each of the breakdown elements, a brief synopsis should be provided on where that element of the project is supposed to be as of the meeting and where it actually is. Because the number of elements in a large project may count in the dozens at any given point in time, the reporting structures for these meetings may be (of necessity) very rigid and formal.

Sample Status Meeting Agenda

Participants: (Names/Organizations)

Date:

Time:

Place:

1.0   Project Overview

The project overview should be provided by the project manager or her designee. It should be a brief analysis of areas of significant accomplishment and shortfall.

2.0   Individual Status Reports

2.1   Component Status Report
   2.1.1   Targeted accomplishments
   2.1.2   Actual accomplishments
   2.1.3   Variance analysis
   2.1.4   Action items
2.2   ...

The individual status reports should be structured to ensure the succinct sharing of information. Each team member providing a report should be directed to share only information as prescribed for their individual project element or component (e.g., if they're working on Control Account 1.3.4, they should only provide information on Control Account 1.3.4, and not other components of the WBS). Action items should include the specific support or actions required to bring the component back into alignment with the original targets.

3.0   Action Item Review

The project manager should summarize the action items gathered during the meeting and provide a synopsis of those requirements. These will ultimately be logged on the action item register (Chapter 5).

### Approaches

Some project managers may incorporate the specific timing for each of the agenda items to provide a sense of clarity and comfort for the attendees. By letting the participants know how long each element will be discussed, it affords some insight into their relative level of importance or concern. Project managers in status meetings should focus on only the items on the agenda if it is to be perceived as a credible document in the long term.

### Considerations

The agenda for status meetings may, plausibly, be identical from meeting to meeting, since the approach, the project, and the issues under discussion are frequently the same. The regular intervals at which status meetings should be held are sometimes dictated contractually, but more often are the function of organizational habit. The project manager may want to shift the frequency of the meetings based on project performance, duration, team input, or personal preference. Although those are reasonable considerations, consistency is important. Early notification of any change in status meeting protocol is essential if a sense of consistency has been achieved.

## Status Reports

### Purpose

Organizations use status reports to provide managers, customers, and team members with an understanding of where projects stand as of a given data date in terms of schedule, cost, scope, and any other predefined issues of significance. They are not intended to explore the efforts applied to achieve the current status, but only to afford a picture of the current project condition.

### Application

Status reports are used in results-driven organizations, where a high level of importance is put on degrees of achievement, rather than on the project history or the level of effort. They may be used in conjunction with, or as a supplement to, other types of progress reports, but on their own, they are intended only to reflect project standing as of a given point in time. As with other measurement reports, they should be initially developed and formatted as early in the project as possible and applied as a component of the controlling processes.

### Content

As with many types of project reporting, status reports can be provided at differing levels of depth for different audiences. Because many status reports are directly tied to the work breakdown structure (Chapter 4), the different levels of depth in the

WBS can be tied to different status report audiences. For team members, for example, the work package level of the WBS may provide the structure they require in terms of status reports. Augmented by supporting information regarding degrees of completion and/or acceptance, the WBS at the work package level becomes their status report, a sample of which is shown in Table 6.8.

Although managers may be tempted to provide more in-depth information, that is normally embedded in a progress report, rather than a status report. The status report's intent is one of sharing high-level information on where the project stands at a given point in time.

### Approaches

Because the information can easily be tied to the WBS, status reports are often most easily developed within the project management software packages. Although some packages have preformed templates and printouts on project status, customized tables are easy to build in most packages to accommodate the specific needs of the organization. By rolling the WBS up to the appropriate reporting level, the status report built within the project management software becomes far more utilitarian.

### Considerations

Because status reports do not provide the background and history of the problems that may drive a project from perfect performance, some project managers are reticent to use status reports in their pure form. They instead prefer to have the opportunity to sanitize some of the data and to provide a rationale as to why certain tasks or deliverables are in the state they're in. In those environments, progress reports are more appropriate.

## Summary Reports

### Purpose

Summary reports grant insight on the current standing of individual or multiple projects within an organization and the overall health of those projects, their teams,

**Table 6.8** Sample Status Report

| WBS Code | Title | Status |
|----------|-------|--------|
| 1.5.4 | Control Account | |
| 1.5.4.1 | Work Package | Late/on plan/early |
| | | Over budget/on plan/under budget |
| | | Not started/begun |
| | | Complete/accepted |
| 1.5.4.2 | Work Package | Late/on plan/early |
| | | Over budget/on plan/under budget |
| | | Not started/begun |
| | | Complete/accepted |
| 1.5.4.3 | Work Package | Late/on plan/early |
| | | Over budget/on plan/under budget |
| | | Not started/begun |
| | | Complete/accepted |

and their customer relationships. They are used by senior management to conduct general assessments of individual projects and to ascertain the overall well-being of the project portfolio. Summary reports are used by project managers to maintain a perspective on the multiple projects to which they are assigned.

### Application

Summary reports provide general overview information on projects to determine which projects are in trouble, which require greater attention and which are forging ahead under their own power. They are brief synopses of the projects in terms of time, cost, and scope that allow for "big picture" analysis. Because summary reports are evaluation tools, they should be developed early in the project to ensure the proper metrics are measured during the project life cycle.

### Content

Portfolio summary reports incorporate only high-level information about projects, including that shown in Table 6.9.

In a portfolio summary report, much of the information may be directly imported from the project management software or from earned value analysis reports. By using percentages for the triple constraint aspects of the report, apples-to-apples comparisons can be made across multiple projects.

Project summary reports expand that same information slightly, but still maintain a very high-level, one-page perspective (Table 6.10).

### Approaches

The determination to use the project or portfolio summary report is largely driven by the desired output or use of those reports. If the reviewer is interested only in a single project, then the latter table is more appropriate. If, however, the expectation is to review all of the projects in a functional or organizational portfolio, then a listing of the multiple projects (rather than a page-by-page analysis) will be more effective.

### Considerations

Summary reports, are by their nature, short. They are not intended to provide in-depth information. Some individuals will attempt to augment the summary report in an effort to get more detail. Normally, that information is available in other report types (e.g., progress or status reports).

**Table 6.9**   Sample Portfolio Summary Report

| Report produced by: | | | | | | |
|---|---|---|---|---|---|---|
| Date of analysis: | | | | Data current as of: | | |
| Project Name/Owner | Schedule Variance Percentage | Cost Variance Percentage | Tasks % Complete | Resource Hours Planned | Resource Hours Consumed | Potential Jeopardy Issues |
| | | | | | | |
| | | | | | | |

**Table 6.10**  Sample Project Summary Report

| Project Name: | | | |
|---|---|---|---|
| Date of analysis: | | Data current as of: | |
| Current planned completion date: | | Current target completion budget: | |
| Original target completion date | | Original target completion budget: | |
| Completion date variance: | | Completion budget variance: | |
| Tasks under way: | | Tasks complete: | |
| Tasks planned to be under way: | | Tasks planned to be complete: | |

## Team Report

### Purpose

The term *team report* actually refers to two types of standard reporting, only one of which will be discussed here. Team reports refer both to any report generated by an organized team and to a report focused on the status, performance, integration, and effectiveness of the team itself. For the sake of this discussion, the focus is on the latter. The purpose of these team reports is to affirm for management that the team is functioning as a working whole toward its assigned goal.

### Application

Team reports are used early in projects to let management know that the team is performing to expectation, and later in the project (particularly with troubled teams) to reassure management that the same level of efficacy that was expected is being achieved.

### Content

A team report will list the roles and responsibilities of the individual team members and will identify their respective level of involvement or commitment (Table 6.11). In addition to the specific roles of the individual team members, the team report will provide an overview paragraph regarding team performance, including any outstanding management support issues or any commitments that are not currently being met. The report will also include recommendations regarding future team support or performance.

In Table 6.11, the Tuckman model team performance assessment component refers to the model of group development created by Bruce Tuckman [1] in 1965 in which teams are sorted into their relative development levels as *forming, storming, norming,* and *performing.* Project managers with some organizational development

**Table 6.11**   Sample Team Report

| Project Team Report | | | | |
|---|---|---|---|---|
| Project name: | | Project manager name/contact information: | | |
| Team member name | Title (both organizational and project) | Role (project only) | Commitments in the next 2 weeks | Percent of time committed to the project |
| | | | | |
| | | | | |
| | | | | |
| | | | | |
| Team Status | | | | |
| Project tasks % complete | | Team performance assessment (per Tuckman): | Forming Storming Norming Performing Adjourning | |
| Project tasks scheduled % complete | | Rationale for team performance assessment | | |
| Team members departing project in the next month: | | | | |
| Team members joining project in the next month: | | | | |

experience will be able to intuitively identify the team stage, whereas those without can use the following scale to determine where the team fits within the model:

*Forming*—still getting to know one another and more focused on the individual, rather than the role in the project.

*Storming*—mapping out roles and responsibilities both for the project and in team dynamics.

*Norming*—working within established roles and responsibilities, but focusing largely on individual roles and duties, rather than the team.

*Performing*—Working within established roles and responsibilities, sharing insight and information, and facilitating each other's roles.

Because Tuckman's model is a standard of organizational development, it provides a common frame of reference by which to evaluate team performance.

### Approaches

The team report is drafted by the project manager and provides a human resources perspective that is sometimes lost in the project environment. By generating reports about the influx of new team members or the shifting roles and responsibilities, it is possible in some cases to diagnose team behavioral problems and to facilitate resolution.

### Considerations

Because the team report relates directly to individual performance, some team members will challenge it. They may have concerns about their title, roles, or responsibilities as documented in the report. The project manager should anticipate such objections and should strive to keep the report descriptions as objective as is humanly possible.

## Variance Report

### Purpose

The variance report (also known as an exception report) identifies areas where the project has strayed from its original objectives, approaches, or targets and the degree to which such variance exists. It also provides a documentary history of the rationale for any variance.

### Application

Variance reports are particularly common in organizations that use management by exception as their preferred management approach. The variance report identifies those areas where exceptions have occurred, allowing for clear management attention to those areas for expedited resolution.

### Content

A variance report will present the type of information under consideration (e.g., cost, schedule, contract line items) from both the original project plan perspective and the current status perspective, followed by a commentary on why the two do not match. Some variance reports will also include a recovery plan for the exceptions. Tables 6.12, 6.13, and 6.14 provide examples of variance reports.

### Approaches

The nature of the organization and its cultural attitude toward cost, schedule, and scope variance may largely drive the type of exception report developed. The approach may also be driven by the availability of information, because actual costs may be elusive in some organizations. The key selection criteria for a particular type of variance report should be its ability to drive the organization to specific, actionable behaviors. If the variance cannot be acted on, there is limited utility to developing the documentation.

### Considerations

Variance reports may draw information from a variety of sources, but the commentary provided with a variance report should be developed independent of the other sources. The commentary should reflect the project manager's assessment of the information in the report, unless there are attachments to provide any supplemental insights the project manager used in the commentary.

**Table 6.12**   Budget Variance Report Example

| Project Name: | | | | | |
|---|---|---|---|---|---|
| Project Manager: | | | Reporting Date: | | |
| Activity/ Deliverable | Budgeted | Actual | Variance | Percentage | Comment |
| | | | | | |
| | | | | | |

**Table 6.13**   Schedule Variance Report Example

| Project Name: | | | | | |
|---|---|---|---|---|---|
| Project Manager: | | | Reporting Date: | | |
| Activity/Deliverable | Planned Finish | Targeted or Actual Finish | Variance | Percentage | Comment |
| | | | | | |
| | | | | | |

**Table 6.14**   Deliverable/Activity Variance Report Example

| Project Name: | | | | |
|---|---|---|---|---|
| Project Manager: | | | Reporting Date: | |
| Activity/Deliverable | Original Specification | Actual/Final Specification | Nature of Variance | Comment |
| | | | | |
| | | | | |

## Conclusion

In the controlling processes, the primary objective is to stay the course on which a project is supposed to go. The focus of most of the tools is to either serve that objective or to ensure that there is awareness when that objective is not being met. These tools should be deployed in that context.

## Reference

[1]   Tuckman, B., "Developmental Sequence in Small Groups," *Psychological Bulletin*, Vol. 63, 1965, pp. 384–399.

## CHAPTER 7

# Communications Tools in the Closing Processes

In the closing processes, the communications tools generally focus on ensuring an historic record of what the project accomplished and how it was accomplished. There is also a tendency to generate documents intended to affirm that the best possible efforts were put forth and that any anomalies were the result of specific causes, rather than the processes themselves. In the closing processes, the documentation takes on heightened significance, because it is often required in order to get customer acceptance, and yet the documentation is not generally ripe for amendment or correction because it represents the "final" version of whatever was originally generated.

## As-Built Drawings

### Purpose

As-built drawings are the graphic historic record of the final deliverables of a project. In a construction effort, they are the amended blueprints, reflecting the project as it finally evolved. In a process development effort, they may be a final flowchart, depicting how the process will be implemented from this point forward. They are used to create a final visual depiction of the project in its constructed state to ensure that those who must deal with the project deliverables in the future know and understand how the final deliverables looked at completion.

### Application

As-built drawings are rare among closing documents, in that they are frequently accessed after the project is complete. They are used by a variety of individuals to ensure they understand how the project's deliverables can be used during the utilization stage. In construction, for example, they become essential for identifying where concrete was poured, where electrical and plumbing lines are nestled, and where access to certain features can be achieved. In a process effort, the drawings become important for identifying how any modifications to the process may ripple through the entire process and how the remaining process steps may be affected. In any design effort, the as-built drawings provide clarity on the final iteration of the design so future workers can understand the nature of and cause for any design changes that may have occurred since the project was conceived.

### Content

As the name implies, the as-built drawings are made up of graphic representations of the final project deliverables. Such representations may range from drawings of buildings to electrical schematics to process flow diagrams. The drawings should include some consistent elements, however. They should have a reference code to indicate the original project name, number, or other code to identify where to find the document within the organization's filing system. They should have a date to reflect when they were generated (and if they supersede any earlier versions). Because "as-built" may fluctuate in the waning days of a project, a reference date is crucial, particularly for efforts in which the final days include a number of last-minute modifications. If the as-built drawing is one of a set of multiple drawings, the names and locations of the related documents should also be identified.

In addition to the drawing itself, the documentation should also include the names and locations of any standards referenced on the drawing.

### Approaches

Because as-built drawings reflect the final version of the project deliverables, they take time to develop. But since they are at the end of the project, there is often a temptation to begin developing such drawings before the total effort is complete—and that's not an unreasonable or inappropriate temptation. The key, however, is to accept the level of rework that will invariably be associated with initiating the work early.

A similar problem occurs when trying to build new as-built drawings, using the old version as the primary reference. A classic episode occurred at one U.S. Pentagon project where the team went to a set of as-built drawings in the 1990s and found that they had not been updated since shortly after World War II. As a result, many of the references in the drawings were completely out of date, and a significant level of effort was invested in retracing what should have been updated with every modification over the years.

### Considerations

Different people will have different perceptions about when a project is sufficiently complete to craft the final as-built drawings. Ideally, such a determination should be made at the project's inception and built into the WBS, so there is clarity on when the effort should be under way (and thus what it will or will not affect).

Another key consideration is the level of depth for the drawings. If they are crafted from a very high-level perspective, limited change will be required if minor modifications occur in the waning days of the project. If they are crafted in excruciating detail, the project deadline may need to be extended.

## Closeout Meeting Agenda/Key Review Meeting Agenda

### Purpose

Project closeout meetings, like project kickoff meetings, may be internal or external. The external closeout meeting is designed to affirm that the customer's deliverables have been produced and accepted, while the internal closeout meeting is designed to ensure that administrative issues have been addressed and that the organizational resources are free to return to their other duties. The agenda for each must be modified to serve the proper purpose.

## Application

The meetings are used to minimize the probability that outstanding project issues will surface at a later date, when resources are no longer available for the project within the organization. They are used with the customer to serve as a finalizing act, asserting that after the meeting issues are addressed, the project will be formally closed out. The agenda for such meetings should be forwarded to the customer and/or the team well in advance of the meeting to allow time for changes and alternatives to be presented. Because the meeting is a formal act (often contractually required), the agenda is subject to review prior to use.

## Content

Closeout meetings and their agendas should be focused on acceptance. The content of the meeting should be directed on affirming that all work packages within the WBS have been closed and that all of the deliverables have been properly forwarded to the customer. External closeout meetings may also include an effort to get the customer's signature on acceptance documents. The external closeout meeting is normally held prior to the internal closeout meeting.

Sample External Closeout Meeting Agenda

Participants: (Names/Organizations)

(This will include the internal or external customer, as well as key team members to field questions regarding project performance or outcomes.)

Date:

Time:

Place:

1.0   Project Overview

The project overview should be provided by the project manager or his designee. It should be a brief analysis of what has been delivered to the customer.

2.0   Synopsis of Deliverables

The synopsis should include detail on who the deliverables were transferred to and who acknowledged acceptance. Any deviations from specifications should be clearly identified, as well as the authority who accepted the deviations.

3.0   Project Acceptance

If the customer (internal or external) has not already done so, she should be asked to sign project acceptance documentation. This will either finalize the project or raise any last-minute issues for resolution. If there are last-minute issues, the project manager may draft an amendment to the acceptance document indicating that when the final action items are addressed, the project will be considered "accepted" by the customer.

## 4.0   Next Steps

In most project relationships, there are opportunities for follow-on work or supplemental activity associated with the project. If those opportunities exist (or may exist), the project manager should identify them during the closeout meeting for further action.

## 5.0   Action Item Review

The project manager should summarize the action items gathered during the meeting and provide a synopsis of those requirements. These will ultimately be logged on the action item register (Chapter 5).

### Sample Internal Closeout Meeting Agenda

Participants: (Names/Organizations)

(This will not include the customer, but should include key team members from all aspects of the project. Depending on the project culture, project subcontractors may or may not be invited to participate.)

**Date:**

**Time:**

**Place:**

## 1.0   Project Overview

The project overview should be provided by the project manager or his designee. It should be a brief analysis of what has been delivered to the customer and the success of the approach.

## 2.0   Synopsis of Deliverables

This should include detail on who the deliverables were transferred to and who acknowledged acceptance. Any deviations from specification should be clearly identified, as well as the authority who accepted the deviations.

## 3.0   Project Lessons Learned

The project manager or a facilitator should lead the group in developing lessons learned (see later section).

## 4.0   Next Steps

In most project relationships, there are opportunities for follow-on work or supplemental activity associated with the project. If those opportunities exist (or may exist), the project manager should identify them and identify the resources whomay or may not participate in any supplemental activity.

5.0   Action Item Review

The project manager should summarize the action items gathered during the meeting and provide a synopsis of those requirements. These will ultimately be logged on the action item register (Chapter 5).

### Approaches

Every project has some measure of success. A key component of the project closeout meeting is to identify that success. Even projects where relations with the customer have been tortured include some aspects that can be deemed successful. Closing with success in both the internal and external closeout meetings builds the hope that project team members and customers will want to continue the relationship with the project manager and the project organization.

### Considerations

It is sometimes difficult to retain team members long enough to participate in the closeout activities associated with a project. Incentives directly associated with closeout participation are sometimes the only way to ensure they will still be available for the experience. Also, because such meetings come at a time when most of the compelling project work has been completed, a sense of ennui can sometimes take over. The project manager's role as cheerleader is rarely as important as it is at the project closeout meeting. Ending projects on a positive note serves to affirm team member contributions as well as customer wisdom in selecting the project organization in the first place.

## Final Report

### Purpose

Although the final report normally includes a wealth of information, its actual purpose is to draw conclusions about the project, the deliverables, and overall performance. It provides a documentary summary of what happened in synopsis format to allow for quick management, customer, or stakeholder analysis of how the project went.

### Application

The final report is most often provided to management or the customer as one of the last project deliverables. As a summary document, it is sometimes used as one of the means to declare a project officially done. It may also be used to persuade or convince end users or others that the outcomes of the project have merit or that the outcomes of the project will affect or influence their environment in one way or another.

### Content

The final report is a status or progress report for a project that has been completed or abandoned. As such, the content should be a succinct discussion that takes into account the intended path of the project and how work progressed along (or divergent from) that path. The final report should highlight major accomplishments and should, as practicable, provide some space for more extended narrative analysis of the overall effort (Table 7.1).

The only other element that may be included in a final report regularly is a clear conclusion about the project, its outcome, or its effect. Conclusions are commonplace and provide an opportunity to present assertions that may not have been appropriate or defensible during project development.

## Approaches

The final report becomes the authoritative document to present ultimate project performance information. Because of that, and because if often becomes the only major surviving document in the archive, the depth to which it is written and the insights shared become crucial. It may be crafted by a single individual (to present a cohesive

**Table 7.1**   Sample Final Report

| Final Report | | | | | | |
|---|---|---|---|---|---|---|
| Project Name: | | Project Manager: | | | Final Report Date: | |
| **Project Summary Information** | | | | | | |
| Project Start Date: | | Original Planned Completion: | | Actual Completion Date: | | |
| Project Total Budget: | | Project Contingency: | | Contingency Consumed: | | Actual Final Cost: |
| **Executive Summary:** Highlights here should include significant individual and team accomplishment, as well as a summary of why schedule and/or cost variances may exist. Any customer concerns should be incorporated here as well. | | | | | | |
| **Project Detail Information** | | | | | | |
| Deliverable/ Activity | Scheduled Start | | Planned Completion | Actual Start | Actual Completion | Rationale |
| | | | | | | |
| | | | | | | |
| **Outstanding Issues** | | | | | | |
| Issue Unresolved | Impact | | | Response Strategy | Owner | Status/ Outcome |
| | | | | | | |
| | | | | | | |
| | | | | | | |
| | | | | | | |
| **Comments:** | | | | | | |

perspective), but approved by a larger body (either the original project team or their management). Because much of the lesser documentation will be lost, any outstanding or noteworthy performances should be acknowledged in this document. Also, any dramatic learnings may be captured here as well.

### Considerations

The key consideration in crafting a final report is whether or not the report will truly be accepted as final. If there are issues of contention, some individuals may perceive the final report as more of an interim assessment, and want to press for resolution before accepting it. Others will see it as a step to a future "final report" or as a component of a larger set of issues being examined organizationally. Even so, the final report should be treated as though it will be the last word on the project and, in some cases, the only captured documentation.

## Final Variance Analysis

### Purpose

The final variance analysis provides the project manager, team, and management with a comprehensive view of the project in its as-built status to serve as both an update and a historic record of overall project performance.

### Application

The final variance analysis is used internally in some cases as a component of a project manager or team performance report. It also serves as a key component of the final project record.

### Content

The final variance analysis takes on many of the same forms and formats as variance reports (Chapter 6), but normally includes a more extensive narrative at the end of the report to capture the environment and the history that led to the variances (regardless of whether they are positive or negative).

The only version of the final variance analysis that takes on a distinctively different look from the standard variance report is the deliverable/activity variance report. In reporting on deliverables or levels of effort, the final variance analysis focuses on the integrated whole of the project, rather than the component parts. Here again, there will be quite a bit more narrative explaining the nature of the differences between the as-built or as-performing condition of the project's deliverables in contrast with the original plan. As-built drawings are sometimes included (often referenced) as a component of the final variance analysis.

### Approaches

The final variance analysis should incorporate a candid discussion of those elements that went well and those that could have been improved on the project. In writing the final variance analysis, the focus should be on the triple constraint (time, cost, and requirements) and the deviations that occurred and the rationale for those deviations. The emphasis should be on why variance occurred and how it could have been avoided (for future "best practice" analyses).

### Considerations

These analyses may take on the organizational role of affixing blame to one department, division, or individual. That is never their intent. The documents serve the organization most effectively when they build a case for improved practices and protocols in the future. The only way they can achieve that is by clearly documenting the nuances of the existing practices that led to less-than-optimal performance and identifying how those pitfalls could be avoided in the future.

## Formal Acceptance Document

### Purpose

The formal acceptance document captures the concurrence of the customer, sponsor, and other stakeholders that the project has been completed and meets its objectives. The most common form of formal acceptance document is the customer acceptance document, acknowledging that the project has been developed as the customer originally requested.

### Application

Formal acceptance is used as the legal acknowledgment that the project deliverables have been delivered as intended. It is used to certify the project as complete and to release the project organization from any future obligations. Because of the important and heavily contractual nature of the document, it is normally developed early in the project and reviewed with the customer. It is then preserved and used during the phase or project closeout processes.

### Content

A formal acceptance document may be presented as a form or a letter. It will provide detail on the date of origin of the project, the project name, and the degree (if not total) of acceptance. In that the document requires a customer signature and is normally initiated by the project organization, it must be designed to ultimately cycle back to the project organization after being signed. It may reflect any interim or milestone acceptance documents that have been exchanged, but should serve as the ultimate determinant that the customer accepts the deliverables as generated.

> {Customer}
> This letter is to certify that all deliverables under project [name/number] have been delivered in accordance with the contract/agreement dated [date]. Interim approvals for these deliverables were accepted and signed on [dates]. This serves as affirmation that the latest and final deliverables under the project agreement have been conveyed, and we seek your concurrence.
>
> If there are any outstanding issues or concerns that have not been addressed

please alert [name] of our organization as soon as possible. We have appreciated serving you in this effort and look forward to our ongoing relationship. Please sign two copies of this letter, keeping one for your records and returning the other to us via the enclosed self-addressed, stamped envelope.

[Signature]
X_____ (Signature of Customer)
Date_____

### Approaches

Note that the customer acceptance letter does not go into a great deal of detail about the nature of the relationship, the type of work that was being performed, the level of effort, or the specifics of the project. In a formal acceptance document, the key is to reference a primary documentation source (like the contract) and to garner the customer signature. Some customers may perceive any supplements to the formal acceptance document as contractual addenda or as their approval or acceptance of certain behaviors or performance aspects that were not specified within the contract or project agreement.

As to the choice of a letter or form for formal acceptance, the letter creates more of a sense of professional warmth, whereas forms may be perceived as cold or pragmatic. Both serve the same function, but the nature of the relationship or corporate protocols may drive the use of one versus the other.

### Considerations

Because the formal acceptance document requires a commitment on the part of the customer, and because that commitment releases the project organization from further obligations (except for those outlined in the contract), some customers may use the issuance of the formal acceptance document as an opportunity to extract last-minute concessions from the project organization. It is important to note that the acceptance document reflects the project as contracted, and although organizations may choose to accede to the customer's late requests, any major shifts in project approach or delivery may need to be acknowledged as either contract addenda or within the body of the formal acceptance document.

## Lessons Learned Report

### Purpose

Lessons learned are used at midpoints of the project and at project completion to catalog significant new understandings that have evolved as a result of the project. They are used to build the knowledge base of an organization and to establish a history of best and worst practices in project implementation and customer relations.

### Application

Lessons learned should be applied across the organization to facilitate consistency. They should be used and reused as new projects evolve with concerns similar to those addressed by the original lesson learned.

## Content

Lessons learned include detailed, specific information about behaviors, attitudes, approaches, forms, resources, or protocols that work to the benefit or detriment of projects. They are crafted in such a way that those who read them will have a clear sense of the context of the lesson learned, how and why it was derived, and how, why, and when it is appropriate for use in other projects. Lessons learned represent both the mistakes made on projects and the newer "tricks of the trade" identified during a project effort.

The content of a lesson learned report should be provided in context, in detail, and with clarity on where and how it may be implemented effectively (Table 7.2). Because lessons learned are often maintained in a corporate database, the lesson learned documentation will frequently include searchable keywords appropriate to the project and the lesson.

## Approaches

Although forms, databases, and simple documentation are the norm for documenting lessons learned, the approaches to cataloging the information can vary widely. Some organizations capture lessons learned in on-line cartoons and captioned scenarios. Others post lessons learned in hallways and project war rooms. Most capture lessons learned in simple document files or databases. The storage medium is not nearly as important as ensuring that the content includes detailed, in-context information about why the lesson was deemed important enough to store and what specific action can be taken to implement the lesson on future projects.

## Considerations

Storing lessons learned information is one critical consideration, but equally important is the establishment of protocols to ensure access to the information on a consistent basis. Lessons learned may be captured and logged in depth, but if they are not accessed by project managers in the future, they do not serve any real function. Access may be encouraged through creative documentation approaches (like

**Table 7.2**  Sample of a Lessons Learned Report

*Project Title Lessons Learned*

| Lesson learned | Context | Keywords | Owner/Resource Name |
|---|---|---|---|
| Example: Accounting will require Form 421A for all foreign transactions, including Canadian ones. | The project team failed to fill out the form, assuming that since the Regina, SK, office was linked to Minneapolis, no currency exchange form would be required. The project payments to vendors were delayed by 4 weeks. | Accounting, Canada, currency, exchange, international, foreign | John Doe, Project Manager johnd@projectstuff.com |
| *Example:* Acme Enterprises appreciates vendors who use the Acme card for project transactions, and considers it a major step toward customer goodwill. | One team member's charges came in on an Acme card early in the project, and the client acknowledged the transaction in a meeting, praising us for "knowing the customer." The rest of the team applied for Acme cards before the week was over. | Acme, credit, charge, card | Jane Doe, Project Manager janed@projectstuff.com |

cartoons), physical location (hallways and project war rooms), or by including the mandate to access lessons learned as a key component of the performance criteria for project managers and team members.

## Phase Closeouts

### Purpose

The phase closeout documentation is actually a subset of the formal project acceptance, in that the practices are largely the same, but the emphasis is not on project acceptance, but affirmation that a single phase or stage has been completed. Phase closeout documentation captures the concurrence of the customer, sponsor, and other stakeholders that the phase has been completed and meets its objectives.

### Application

Phase closeouts are used to stagger the acceptance process and to facilitate the long-term whole-project closeout process. By gaining acceptance in stages, the project manager may avoid "runaway" projects by knowing if any variance exceeds the norm at a given phase review (rather than waiting until the project is supposed to be complete in its entirety). Whether internal or external, the phase review is used to certify the phase as complete and to release the project team from any future obligations associated with activities in that particular phase.

### Content

Phase closeout documentation is often a component of a larger project methodology and is often presented as a form (Table 7.3). It will provide detail on the date of origin of the project, the project name, and the degree (if not total) of acceptance. Depending on the nature of the methodology, the document may require a customer signature and/or a sponsor signature. It may reflect any milestones that have been achieved, but generally focuses on deliverables or specific checklist items mandated by the organization.

### Approaches

Phase closeout forms are often components of larger methodologies and normally tie directly to the methodology they serve. Although they vary in terms of levels of detail and format, the approach is relatively consistent. They are completed as a phase draws to a close to ensure that there is no cause to revisit stages within that particular phase.

### Considerations

Some forms used for phase closeout go into excruciating detail regarding the specific methodology steps that should have been followed during the course of the project. The ideal would be to avoid micromanagement while still ensuring consistent levels of completion and the ability to ascertain whether a phase is truly complete or not. It is also important to note (as was addressed at the beginning of

**Table 7.3** Sample Phase Closeout Report

| Project Title: | | PHASE CLOSEOUT | |
|---|---|---|---|
| Date Initiated: | / / | Date of Report: | / / |
| Phase Complete: | Initiation<br>Design<br>Development<br>Implementation<br>Termination<br>(circle one) | Phase Acceptance Authority: | Name:<br><br>Contact Information: |
| Phase Requirements | | | |
| Internal authorization form(s) signed | | | ☐ Date: / / |
| Methodology steps complete | | | ☐ Date: / / |
| Customer deliverables complete | | | ☐ Date: / / |
| Work packages/tasks closed out | | | ☐ Date: / / |
| Project binder updated | | | ☐ Date: / / |
| Management review conducted | | | ☐ Date: / / |
| Exceptions documented | | | ☐ Date: / / |
| Signature | | | ☐ Date: / / |
| X_____ | | | ☐ Date: / / |

Chapter 3) that different organizations have different phases, and the nature of "completion" is going to have different meanings for those different phases.

## Project Archives

### Purpose

The project archives serve as the repository for all formal project documentation. They provide the project manager and the team with a single location to seek out specific documentary elements. It is the proverbial "paper trail" for the project.

### Application

An archive is created in order to minimize the spread of project documentation within organizational tracking systems and to facilitate team member quests for components of the project record.

### Content

In theory, the project archive should house all formal project documents, from the original solicitations or requests for the work through the final acceptance documents. Perhaps the single most significant element of the project archive is its index, which lists the specific documents logged, their creation and amendment dates, and the owner or author of the documentation. A sample index is shown in Table 7.4.

The document information should be as clearly stated as possible. Numbering conventions within a project and across projects should be consistent to preclude a proliferation of searches for documents with the same document identifying number. For documents that are archived virtually, the location of the file should include details on where it is housed on the LAN or Web server. For documents that are physically archived, file locations should be explicit, detailing the exact physical location (including details such as which file drawer).

### Approaches

The archive may also be used as a means to limit the storage life of project data by cataloging the date(s) at which project records may be reviewed and may ultimately be deleted. While some organizations retain project records for decades, others strive to clear out their repositories of information and work to ensure that every document (or collection) has a specific retirement date. Such retirement dates should reflect legal, contractual, and cultural requirements for document retention.

### Considerations

The archive has the potential to become a pack rat's fantasy. In a very short span of time, a poorly administered project archive may include so many documents and versions of documents that it becomes unwieldy. The archive should be limited to documentation that is either current or retained by edict. Any new versions of documents should be acknowledged as such and provide some traceability back to older versions, if the older versions are retained. If the older versions are not retained, the differences in the versions should be clearly documented.

## User Acceptance Documents

### Purpose

Project managers develop user acceptance documents in preparation for more comprehensive project acceptance. As with other acceptance documentation, the earlier it is developed and accepted by the customer and other concerned parties, the better. User acceptance documents identify specific project elements that are used

**Table 7.4** Sample Project Archive Index

| Project Archive Index | | | | | | |
|---|---|---|---|---|---|---|
| Document Number | Document Title | Document Location | Date Created/ Logged | Date of Most Recent Amendment | Owner/Author | Owner/Author Contact Information |
| | | | | | | |
| | | | | | | |

extensively by specific end-user groups and validate that a representative segment of that population has reviewed the elements and deemed them acceptable.

## Application

Perhaps the single most common type of user acceptance document is the results form from *user acceptance tests* (UAT) in the information technologies environment. These tests are a classic example of user acceptance documentation, in that they identify a specific subcomponent of the project to be tested, set down the acceptance criteria, define the environment in which the acceptance is being evaluated, and report both the anticipated and actual results. The data can be used to validate deliverables as acceptable, to capture minor variance, or as a rationale to modify existing deliverables.

## Content

User acceptance in any form will include a narrative explanation of the specific criteria that are being evaluated and the thresholds of what should and should not be deemed acceptable. It will identify the participants in the evaluation and the inputs at their disposal to validate that the project element is performing as anticipated. Any special equipment, personnel, or other support needs will be clearly identified. A clear, step-by-step methodology or evaluation approach should be included, as well as the results of the acceptance evaluation.

        1.0   User Acceptance Evaluation Intent
        2.0   Evaluation Criteria
            2.1   Evaluation Process
            2.2   Objective Metrics
            2.3   Subjective Considerations
        3.0   User Acceptance Environment
            3.1   Participants
            3.2   Inputs
            3.3   Cultural Considerations
            3.4   Hardware/Software Needs
        4.0   Evaluation Outputs

## Approaches

The level of detail embedded in user acceptance documentation will hinge directly on what was agreed to contractually and what is absolutely necessary to deliver an acceptable deliverable. Excessive detail in user acceptance evaluations may lead to "analysis paralysis," while a vague user acceptance approach may lead to incomplete or vague outcomes.

## Considerations

The key consideration in user acceptance is what has agreed on in any project or contract documentation. If no user acceptance is required under the contract, it may still be conducted in order to ease the process of final project acceptance, later in the project. However, when it is not required under contract, the project team may not be obligated to provide the evaluation outputs to the customer.

## Conclusion

At the end of a project or phase, much of the interesting work is already complete and much of the excitement has passed. Ensuring historical documentation at project completion is a challenge in any organization. The tools included in this chapter help to ensure consistency at a time when team members' performance is sometimes at its most inconsistent—during the transition from project to project or from phase to phase.

## CHAPTER 8

# Implementing Communications Tools

The tools in this book will be effective only if they are implemented properly. That does not mean to say that they will all be used for their original, intended use. There is always the possibility of finding new and somewhat innovative uses for tools. It is not unlike the crowbar in a workshop that was never intended to be applied as a hammer, but in the right situation, it serves that function. What has been provided here is some guidance on the intended purposes and applications of the tools. To implement them effectively, they need to be reassessed in the context of the organization and those who will be using them.

## Stakeholder Considerations

The end users of communications tools are both the senders and receivers of the communications message. As such, all of their needs have to be considered. In some environments, stakeholders are intensely form averse. They will do anything to avoid preordained forms, formats, and protocols. They prefer to see themselves as free agents, capable of determining the appropriate applications at the appropriate times. In a smaller project environment, that may be possible, but it remains a less desirable approach because of the inability to reuse and reapply tools and techniques. Each project becomes a new invention without some consistency.

In determining if preformatted tools should be used with a given set of stakeholders, the following questions should be considered:

- Will this ensure the client/customer a more consistent project experience?
- Is this something that will happen more than once in this project?
- Will the tool lead to a better understanding of the information to be communicated?
- Is the amount of time required to learn the tool less than the amount of time to create, share, and store the message ad hoc?

If the answers to all of these questions are "no," then a case may be made for a less rigid communications approach. If any of the answers are "yes," then a sound rationale exists for applying the tool.

Some stakeholders will invariably balk at the notion of formatted communications tools. They may feel that the forms and formats inhibit, rather than encourage, communications. For those with that objection, it may be helpful to identify what components of the forms or formats they find objectionable and to explore why.

The information may be seen as redundant or unnecessary. They may not understand why a particular informational element needs to be tied to this particular communication. They may be viewing the entire experience through their own prism, rather than in the greater organizational context.

## Organizational Considerations

Organizations have significant informational needs, and not all of them are readily understandable or apparent. Some are rooted in historic concerns, whereas others are grounded in legal requirements. Many of these requirements are not apparent to individual stakeholders in a project. The stakeholders do not necessarily know (or need to know) the history that has driven the organization to a particular communications approach. However, the project manager should be aware of and attuned to the rationale for the communications tools. That means that he should ask questions when certain tools are required:

- How long has this communications tool been applied?
- When was it first applied and why?
- Does that rationale still exist?
- Are there alternative means to gather, share, and archive the information required?
- Are those alternatives potentially more onerous than the current approach?

The answers to those questions afford the project manager a viable defense for applying virtually any of the tools in this toolkit. The longevity question is important, because it may illustrate how the tool has served the organization over time, *or* that the tool is not something from "days of old," but that reflects a current need. By knowing the organization history, or even the project history, behind the application of a particular tool, the project manager can effectively deflect criticism and educate others on how and why tools are being applied.

## Verbal Communication

Most of the tools in the text are written tools. Only a few of those identified are verbal. But none of these tools can be applied isolated from verbal communication. Verbal communications support the other tools, just as the other tools frequently support verbal communications. For virtually all verbal communications in the project environment, some form of postdiscussion documentation can be appropriate. Verbal communications may be formal or informal, but should not be discounted just because they are verbal, rather than written. Promises made verbally are just as legally binding (but harder to prove) than those that are written. Verbal communications are frequently the "glue" that binds a project's disparate communications elements together.

### Informal Verbal Communication

Informal verbal communications are conducted to ensure the day-to-day operations of the project are moving ahead as planned. They are generally uncontrolled and unmonitored, but that does not mean that they are unimportant. As discussed in Chapter 2 on ad hoc conversations, there is still a need to ensure that these conversations (particularly when they involve customer, client, or sponsor personnel) are limited in scope. Whenever the conversations stray into commitments to a customer, reallocation of resources, modification of contractual arrangements, or anything requiring formal approval, the conversation should be redirected to a more formal setting (such as a meeting). Other limitations (such as limitations on the nature of conversations about other project stakeholders) may be ordained by the project team, but may be far more difficult to enforce.

Limiting informal verbal communication is not dictatorial. It is a necessity of project life to discriminate between what the organization is committing to and what it is not.

### Formal Verbal Communications

Formal verbal communications are generally far more constrained and controlled. Because they are normally planned out carefully, there is less chance that a casual remark will be misconstrued. As discussed earlier in the text, these can take on the form of conference calls, customer presentations, meetings, and virtually any type of preplanned project gathering.

Some common aspects of such communication are that the sender in the communications model must speak clearly and should ensure that the receivers have no significant filters that may inhibit communication. If a team member speaks only French, for example, that is going to inhibit that person's ability to interpret a conference call being conducted in English. The project manager's responsibility in this environment is to eliminate as many of the distractions and filters from the communications model as possible to ensure clear, effective communications. And, because the communication is formal, there is of necessity some postmeeting documentation that should capture what was said and what commitments were made.

## Evaluating Communications Effectiveness

Whether the communication is written or verbal, formal or informal, the question must be asked as to whether or not it was effective. Did the information transfer that had to occur happen? Communications effectiveness can only be tested through feedback—the receiver is the ultimate determinant as to whether or not the message was received. The obvious test of communications effectiveness is to ask the receiver in the communications model to reiterate what has been said or what commitments have been made. Although they may be able to recite chapter and verse of what was originally stated, such regurgitation may not truly reflect understanding. Better instead to ask the receiver how they will act on the information or what the next steps in the process are, to ensure the communication has gone from interpretation to action.

Similarly, with written communication tools, the effectiveness can be measured not by the thoroughness with which they are completed, but by the actions they spur. If they are serving their roles of archive, research tool, legal defense, or call to action, then they are effective. If they have simply become elements of "shelf-ware" with no active future, then it may be time to reconsider their use.

# About the Author

Carl Pritchard is the president of Pritchard Management Associates and is an internationally recognized lecturer and author in project management. Mr. Pritchard has presented seminars and addresses around the world and is the author of multiple texts in project management. He is the U.S. correspondent for a leading project management publication in the United Kingdom, *Project Manager Today*.

As a lecturer, Mr. Pritchard has spoken at each of the last 10 major annual Project Management Institute (PMI) national symposia in the United States and Canada, and he is a regular presenter for PMI's *SeminarsWorld* series, both in the classroom and on-line.

He is active in professional project management associations and is a certified Project Management Professional. Mr. Pritchard has a B.A. in journalism from Ohio State University.

# Index

## Recent Titles in the Artech House
## Effective Project Management Library

Robert K. Wysocki, Series Editor

*The Project Management Communications Toolkit*, Carl Pritchard

*Project Management Process Improvement*, Robert K. Wysocki

For further information on these and other Artech House titles,
including previously considered out-of-print books now available through our
In-Print-Forever® (IPF®) program, contact:

Artech House
685 Canton Street
Norwood, MA 02062
Phone: 781-769-9750
Fax: 781-769-6334
e-mail: artech@artechhouse.com

Artech House
46 Gillingham Street
London SW1V 1AH UK
Phone: +44 (0)20 7596-8750
Fax: +44 (0)20 7630-0166
e-mail: artech-uk@artechhouse.com

Find us on the World Wide Web at:
www.artechhouse.com